DATE DUE

GAYLORD

HIGGLEDY PIGGLEDY GROWTH AGAIN

A. C. RAYNER   I. M. D. LITTLE

HIGGLEDY PIGGLEDY
GROWTH AGAIN

*An Investigation of the Predictability of
Company Earnings and Dividends in the U.K.
1951—1961*

AUGUSTUS M. KELLEY · PUBLISHERS
NEW JERSEY
1971

© BASIL BLACKWELL 1966

Published in the United States by
Augustus M. Kelley · Publishers
Clifton, New Jersey 07012

First Printed 1966
Reprinted 1971

Library of Congress No. 66-73566
ISBN 0 678 06261 7

Printed in Great Britain
by Blackwell's in the City of Oxford and
bound by The Kemp Hall Bindery

FOREWORD

By I. M. D. LITTLE

This book owes its origin to my article of almost the same title in the *Bulletin of the Oxford University Institute of Economics and Statistics*, November 1962. It deals largely (Chapter I) with what was the main subject of the article, whether the past growth performance of a company sheds light on its future: but it also investigates (Chapter II) whether low yielding shares perform better than high yielding shares, and what influence past performance has on the valuation of a share. These are not easy questions to answer. Despite the obvious interest, no one apart from the present authors and Mr. M. F. G. Scott[1], has, so far as I know, tried to answer them for the U.K. This is not as amazing as it sounds. The Company Act of 1948 first forced companies to consolidate their accounts with those of their subsidiaries. Before that, one could not tell what companies earnings were, or how they grew. It is also only since 1951 that Moodies Services Ltd. has undertaken the very laborious work of adjusting dividends and earnings for capital changes. Then several years had to pass before there were enough adjusted consolidated results to permit a statistical analysis. Now I expect that, as the years pass and the evidence accumulates, the present effort may prove to be the first of a series. Our results will certainly bear checking again in a few years time, by others I hope.

Although I have never doubted the main conclusion of my article, which is implicit in its title, Mr. Rayner had some doubts, and so did others. Certainly, the analytic method used was open to some criticism. Mr. Rayner, then a Research Fellow of Nuffield College, agreed to submit the figures to more searching analysis which would, one hoped, confirm or refute my conclusions. This, Mr. Rayner has now done in Chapter I. In presenting his own work, he has skilfully woven in almost the whole of my original article, thus using it as well as transcending it. There is no point in trying to separate what I originally wrote from what he has added, except to say that the more professional the method the more

[1] 'Relative Share Prices and Yields,' *Oxford Economic Papers*, Oct. 1962.

probable it is that Mr. Rayner used it. Chapter II, which is mainly about whether low-yielding shares perform best, is entirely Mr. Rayner's work. I acted only as critic and editor. Chapter III, summarizing other authors' work on stock market price behaviour, is also his. But I would like to say that I happily associate myself with what Mr. Rayner has written: happily, because, where his findings might have differed from my original article, there is in fact agreement.

If, at any point, the reader detects any sign of a failure of that close co-operation which should exist between joint authors, this should be ascribed to the fact that they were not able to meet while the book was in preparation, Mr. Rayner being in Tokyo and myself in Oxford.

Our acknowledgments are due to Mr. M. F. G. Scott who read Chapters I and II and made a number of helpful comments.

We are also obliged to Vickers da Costa and Company, who made their computer freely available to us.

I. M. D. LITTLE,

Nuffield College, Oxford.

CONTENTS

CHAPTER I

THE GROWTH OF EARNINGS

(1) *Introduction*

The main concern of this chapter will be to investigate patterns of the growth of earnings in order to try and discover whether past growth leads to further growth; in other words, whether a successful management continues to do well. This is the content of the main part of the chapter, but there is at the end also a short section on the factors affecting growth.

An apology should be given at this early stage for the fact that this chapter is very much of a hybrid, since it is a combination of work that has already been published in the article 'Higgledy Piggledy Growth' (I. M. D. Little, *op. cit.*) with further work on the same problem done by A. C. Rayner. Thus only part of the results has not been seen before. Also, the time periods covered and the numbers of firms included in the different investigations vary in a rather confusing fashion. The excuse for this is that the further work was an attempt to solve some of the problems that became apparent in the earlier work, rather than an extension of the analysis shown there. The actual differences will be outlined as the chapter progresses.

Before launching into the investigation, it is as well to start by giving some reasons for being interested in growth stability. The first is the one that the market is concerned with, which is that there has been, for the last few years, a belief in the concept of 'growth stocks'. For the privilege of holding these particular stocks, the investor has been willing to forego a considerable amount of income in the belief that their market price would rise in the future. This can continue to happen in a rational market only if past growth is repeated in the future; the market may be able to fool itself for a while, but will insist on some good results relative to the rest of the industry sooner or later. Therefore, with this belief in growth stocks, investors are also expressing a belief that firms which have grown relatively better than others in the past will continue to do so in the future. The rationale for this belief

B

has been, to some extent at least, the argument that good past growth demonstrated good management which could be expected to continue.

The second reason is that, from the point of view of society, it is desirable to have a market mechanism which enables relatively good managements (meaning those which can get a relatively high return on new assets), to borrow on easier terms than bad managements—for this will encourage them to borrow more, and hence to manage more of society's new investment than they would otherwise. But if there is no tendency for good past growth to continue, and the growth (or decline) of companies seems to assume a random pattern, then one of three possibilities must be the case: (1) there is no such thing as good and bad management, (2) the management changes from good to bad and back again, (3) investors have been quite wrong in assuming that good past growth was any indication that the management was handling its assets well, or vice versa. Of these three possibilities, the first seems absurd. The second recalls Marshall's famous analogy of the forest,[1] but Marshall's theory is not really any explanation of our results, given the high frequency of changes from relatively good to relatively bad performance which they show, nor was it intended to refer to public joint-stock companies. The third possibility raises the question of how, if the firm's performance is random, which our results tend to show, there can be any possibility of a rational distribution of new savings to firms. By what else can the market judge, if not by performance? By what else in practice can anyone judge? Finally, how can it be possible for a management, which is getting a higher return on new assets, not to grow faster than those with a lower return? Is the first possibility so absurd after all?

Thus our reasons for being interested are relevant not only to investors' behaviour in the market, but also to economists' appraisals of the function of a stock market in a capitalist society.

(2) The Material

The companies, whose behaviour is investigated in this book, are all charted by Moodies Services, Ltd, in their 'Security Indices and Charts Service'; which covers the U.K. companies that Moodies thinks are of interest to the investing public. This includes all large

[1] Principles, 8th edition, p. 315.

companies, and many of medium size. For parts of this chapter, a second group of companies of smaller size is investigated; these are chosen at random from Moodies Index of Public Companies, with the limitation that their profits in 1951 must not have been more than £250,000. This condition adequately separates the two samples. For both large and small firms to be included in the sample, they had to have complete financial records from 1951 to 1959 or 1961.[1] A complication here is that the sample used has three distinct sizes in the case of the large firms: the largest is that used in the original paper, which is those companies with complete records from 1951–1959, and therefore those companies which were included in Moodies Service in 1951, and avoided bankruptcy and merger until the end of the period. This is the sample used in those results, shown in the earlier paper, which are used again here. The next sample is a little smaller, being those firms which survived in the same way for the further two years to 1961. In fact, only the brewery companies suffered any great loss in these two years, but they lost over a third of their number (by merger) in this short period. This sample is used in this chapter where new work is being presented. The final, and smallest, sample is that used in the next chapter, where figures for the Moodies Services' 'earnings yield ratio' are required as well as those for earnings and dividends, and so a few firms, which had incomplete records for this, had to be eliminated from the larger sample. None of this is of great importance, but it does mean that it is difficult to compare some results directly with others in different parts of the book.

The additional work presented in this chapter is concerned with earnings only, since, in the long run at least, dividends must follow earnings, and, therefore, can only be some sort of smoothed out image of what happens to earnings. If there is no consistent pattern to earnings, then there cannot be one for dividends either, in the long run.

However, as will be discussed at some length in the next chapter, it is not too clear just how closely dividends do follow earnings, since they seem to behave in rather a different fashion at least over a period of several years. Also, the new work included in this chapter, and the following one, ignores the small firms since, as we shall see, they seem to behave in the same way as the larger ones.

---

[1] For some of the correlation analysis, some further firms were included which had records for the relevant years, but not for the whole period.

The sample of large firms consists of all the firms charted by Moodies that fulfil the appropriate conditions for the samples and belong to the following groups:

Breweries.
* Building (including materials, but excluding the sub-industries, 'contractors' and 'road making materials').
* Chemicals and Pharmaceuticals.
Cotton Textiles.
* Electrical Engineering, Radio, and Television.
Food.
* Motors (including components and distributors).
* Mechanical Engineering and Shipbuilding.
Miscellaneous.
* Paper and Printing, Newspapers and Publishers.
Stores.
* Wool, Silk, and Rayon.

Those industries marked with an asterisk are amalgamations of different sections published by Moodies, the purpose of amalgamation being to obtain a reasonably large number of companies in each group. For most of this chapter, and the following one, mechanical engineering is sub-divided into two groups, those firms with accounting dates ending on December 31st, and the rest. This was done since it was the largest group, and therefore it was possible to divide it like this in order to allow for the fact that we would expect some cyclical or chance factors to affect one firm's performance relative to another's if their accounting years differ.

Other groups were excluded because they belong to a different class of industry (banks, hire-purchase, investment trusts, oil, mining and plantations), or because there were both less than 20 firms in the group and it could not be plausibly amalgamated with another (e.g. Steel). The number of firms in each of the samples will be stated when the sample is used for the first time.

The figures used are throughout corrected for scrip and rights issues. This task was undertaken by Moodies.[1]

---

[1] The formula used is as follows: suppose the issue is 1 for n new shares at a price of pr per share, and that the last cum-rights price is pc. Then the correction applied to the pre-issue dividends, earnings, etc. is, $\dfrac{n+1}{n+\dfrac{pr}{pc}}$.

The three types of financial figures which were used to calculate the growth rates are as follows:

(i) Dividends expressed as a percentage of equity capital.

(ii) Earnings, net of interest, taxation, minority interests, and preference dividends (i.e. 'earned for ordinary'), expressed as a percentage of equity capital.

(iii) Pre-tax earnings per £1 nominal of equity capital. In effect, this differs from 'earned for ordinary' only in that it is before tax, and before preference dividends.

Since it was desired to have a figure for the pre-tax earnings that could be conceived of as being that part directly attributable to the ordinary shareholder, it would have been better that the preference dividends should have been subtracted from (iii) above. However, since the amount of preference dividends is usually small, and so unlikely to have much effect on growth rates, and since Moodies had calculated the figures as above, it was decided not to adjust for this.

Apart from the section immediately following, the figures used when calculating earnings growth, in this chapter and the next, have been the pre-tax earnings, the last item in the above list. The reasons for choosing this figure are the following: (1) it was considered that the tax which a company pays in a particular year bears only a loose relation to its liability on current earnings, owing to adjustments in respect of past periods, and this variability would introduce an irrelevant and disturbing influence, (2) with a possibly uneven capital development programme, investment and initial allowances would also introduce variations which would be irrelevant so far as longer term trends were concerned.

Earnings were adjusted for capital changes because (1) variations in earnings caused by the issue of new shares—whether to present shareholders or to others in payment for assets acquired —would also cause haphazard variations in earnings; and more fundamentally because (2) earnings for existing shareholders seem more relevant to an evaluation of a firm's success, not only from the point of view of the investor, but also, on general grounds of economic theory, from the point of view of society as well. This is not meant to imply that the interests of society and the existing shareholders coincide. For instance, it may well benefit society if a good management buys another business by issuing shares, and thereby improves the use of the latters' assets, even at a price which reduces earnings per share. On the other hand, if earnings were not adjusted, a firm could appear remarkably successful merely as a result of acquiring other firms, even if no improvements resulted.

The fact that earnings are pre-tax, whereas dividends must be decided bearing taxation in mind, allows a certain amount of independence in these two variables. This is an observed result in the following chapter, which may be explained in part by the above reason, but much more by the obvious fact that reserves allow directors considerable leeway in deciding dividend rates.

(3). *The Recent History of Earnings and Dividend Growth*

Before getting involved in the process of attempting to find some pattern in growth figures, this section aims to give some general picture of the actual path of growth in the various industries in the period 1951 to 1959 (with some extensions to 1961). Table 1.1 gives the summarised results.

TABLE 1.1
Average Annual Compound Percentage Growth, 1951–59

	Pre-tax Earnings	Earned for Ordinary	Dividends	Retail Prices	Income from employment
441 Large Firms ...	5.1	7.1	11.5	3.8	6.5
81 Small Firms ...	5.8	8.1	7.9		

The figures are obtained by striking an arithmetic average of the ratios of the relevant magnitudes in 1959 to those of 1951, and then reducing this average to an annual compound rate. But a convention had to be adopted to limit the size of the ratios since these can approach infinity where, e.g., a company makes zero or near zero earnings in the base year. The convention adopted was to limit the size of any ratio to 10: that is, a company was not permitted to multiply its earnings or dividends by more than 10 times over the course of the 8 years.[1] Subject to this convention, the significance of, for example, the dividend growth rate is that someone who invested in the large companies so as to obtain an

[1] In the first column of Table 1.1 this convention affected 5 large firms and 4 small firms. In the second column the corresponding figures were 5 and 5: and in the third column 9 and 3.

equal income from each in 1951, and left his holding undisturbed until 1959, would have seen his money income grow at an average annual geometric rate of 11.5 per cent per annum (and similarly at 7.9 per cent per annum for the small companies).

The most notable feature of Table 1.1 is that pre-tax earnings, which are the ultimate long-run prop supporting equity share prices, grew rather slowly for large companies. In real terms they grew by only 1.3 per cent per annum in spite of the fact that the equity shareholder was, as an average over the whole period, having roughly two-thirds of the earnings to which he was entitled ploughed back for him. Neglecting tax changes these savings were, in effect, yielding him only about 2 per cent (tax free).[1] Since a 2 per cent yield on marginal capital seems too low to be plausible, it is likely that the earning power of old assets fell during the period.

'Earned for ordinary' rose rather faster. To a small extent this was due to the gearing element introduced by preference dividends, but mainly it must have been a result of reduced taxation. (In 1951 the rate of tax, excluding allowances, for a company which distributed an average proportion of its profits was 55 per cent: in 1959 the rate was 47.5 per cent, and was not dependent on the proportion distributed). However, the rise in equity shares between these dates (the F.T. index, well known to have been, at least until the last few years, a rather sluggish indicator, rose from December 30th, 1952, to December 30th, 1960, by 164 per cent, an annual compound rate of 12.9 per cent per annum[2] which is very close to the dividend increase) was due mainly to the relaxation of dividends (the average cover fell from 3.9 times in 1951 to 2.3 in 1959), and partly to a general market revaluation of the prospects of equity shares in a period of inflation. In fact, if equity share prices had moved with earnings, and there had been no tax reductions, they would barely have kept pace with inflation in spite of the savings being ploughed back.

[1] £66⅔ of net earnings ploughed back can be roughly associated with a growth in gross real earnings from £100 to £101 6s.—a tax free yield of approximately 2 per cent. Abstracting from tax changes and preference dividends, net earnings attributable to the equity would grow at the same rate as gross earnings.

[2] These dates are selected as ones by which 1951 and 1959 earnings and dividends were known. A company's results are ascribed to e.g. 1951 if the year to which they relate coincides more with the calendar year 1951 than any other. Hence, the so-called 1951 results might not be known until late in 1952; but few 1952 results would be known by then.

The experience of the smaller quoted firms was rather different. Dividends rose by 7.9 per cent per annum, slightly more slowly than 'earned for ordinary' (post tax); while pre-tax earnings and 'earned for ordinary' rose a little faster than those of large companies. Although dividends rose slightly more slowly than 'earned for ordinary' in the case of small companies, the mean dividend cover fell from 3.1 to 2.0. This is superficially paradoxical, but of course quite possible, even apart from the need to introduce conventions when 'earned for ordinary' or the dividend is zero.[1] Table 1.2 gives the performance of the large firms by groups.[2]

TABLE 1.2
Annual Compound Growth Rates 1951–1959

Group	No. of Companies in Group	Pre-tax Earnings %	Earned for Ordinary %	Dividends %
Wool	28	13.2	14.9	7.4
Food	32	10.3	12.6	14.7
Stores	29	6.9	11.1	14.4
Breweries	25	6.0	8.2	7.7
Motors	44	5.5	7.4	12.6
Misc.	48	4.6	6.2	12.8
Building	35	4.3	7.1	10.2
Chemicals	23	4.1	5.3	12.2
Elec. Eng. ...	39	3.8	6.9	11.7
Paper	23	3.0	4.5	10.1
Mech. Eng. ...	91	2.1	3.3	11.4
Cotton	24	−0.7	−0.9	4.7
Average		5.1	7.1	11.5

Ignoring wool and cotton, whose growth rates are peculiarly sensitive to the particular years chosen, it is noticeable that the non-durable consumer-goods and stores are at the top of the list. Apart from paper, those sectors most concerned with investment and exports are at the bottom. Investors are, of course, well aware of this. Food and stores shares have much lower yields than other sectors, with breweries next in spite of their sluggish dividend behaviour.[3] Paper, mechanical engineering,

[1] The convention adopted was to write the cover as zero if 'earned for ordinary' was zero or negative—even if the dividend was zero. If 'earned for ordinary' was positive, but no dividend was paid, the cover was written as 10, which was also used as the limiting value in other cases.

[2] For slightly more detail on the groups see the remarks on the sample on p. 4 above.

[3] This was true when the article was written. Now (August 1964) stores are still among the lowest yielding groups, but building and electrical engineering are more favoured than breweries or food.

and cotton's pre-tax earnings failed to keep pace with the cost of living. Only in wool, food, and stores, did pre-tax earnings' growth exceed the growth in income from employment (6.5 per cent per annum).

Table 1.3 gives the year to year percentage changes of pre-tax earnings by groups for the same 441 firms, together with the geometric means for the whole period. Table 1.4 gives the same figures for dividends.

It is to be noted that the geometric means of the average annual percentage changes differ from the mean compound annual growth rates as given in Table 1.2. The difference is essentially one of weighting. The figures of Table 1.2 are base weighted, that is the weight of each firm is unity in 1951: while those of Table 1.3 and 1.4 are chain-weighted, that is each firm's percentage growth has unit weight in each year. In terms of dividends Table 1.4 shows what would have happened to someone's income who costlessly rearranged his investments to maintain an equal income from each firm. The resultant rate for the whole group is 10.4 per cent per annum—slightly slower than under a no-change policy. The earnings growth for the whole group is 5.0 per cent in Table 1.3 against 5.1 per cent in Table 1.2.

For most individual groups, the dividend growth shown in Table 1.4 is less than that in Table 1.2: but the reverse is true for earnings. One would expect to find that Tables 1.3 and 1.4 would show lower figures if the changes in successive years were positively correlated, since the effective weight of a successful firm is not allowed to increase. The results therefore indicate, so far as earnings go, that there is on balance a slight negative correlation between successive changes. On the other hand the fact that one would have done better, for income, by staying put, indicates that there is some slight positive correlation between successive dividend changes. The connection between changes in earnings from one period to another is examined at length below.

(4) *Does Growth Breed Growth?*

Having got some impression of the overall movements in earnings and dividends, we now move on to the central question in this chapter, which is whether there is any pattern in firms' growth paths, *i.e.*, whether it is possible to predict the future growth of a company by looking at its past results. As stated in the

TABLE 1.3

Average Year to Year Pre-tax Earnings Growth for Large Companies. Percentages

	Brew-eries	Build-ing	Chem-icals	Cotton	Elect. Eng.	Food	Mech. Eng.	Misc.	Motors	Paper	Stores	Wool	Weighted Arith-metic Mean
1952–51	4	– 3	–23	–55	6	3	8	– 9	8	–22	8	– 6	– 3.0
1953–52	12	15	33	26	4	19	– 1	7	4	22	18	36	12.3
1954–53	4	15	17	19	14	19	11	3	18	19	16	10	13.0
1955–54	9	3	2	–23	5	9	13	16	5	1	10	–13	5.5
1956–55	5	2	– 1	4	– 2	15	3	4	–13	– 3	6	12	2.3
1957–56	11	– 3	9	14	– 7	2	2	7	0	6	– 1	– 8	3.3
1958–57	0	– 2	– 5	–51	– 0	7	– 8	– 3	11	5	4	–19	– 4.8
1959–58	7	17	25	26	– 2	12	1	16	25	– 4	0	61	13.3
Geometric Mean	6.4	5.2	5.7	–11.4	4.0	10.7	3.4	4.7	6.5	2.1	6.4	6.5	5.0

TABLE 1.4

Average Year to Year Dividend Growth for Large Companies. Percentages

	Brew-eries	Build-ing	Chem-icals	Cotton	Elect. Eng.	Food	Mech. Eng.	Misc.	Motors	Paper	Stores	Wool	Weighted Arith-metic Mean
1952–51	2	13	2	—1	10	11	11	7	8	3	12	8	8.1
1953–52	7	18	24	21	15	16	15	15	12	18	25	19	16.4
1954–53	6	23	20	14	25	19	23	19	27	29	34	13	22.0
1955–54	4	5	6	—2	5	15	12	7	8	11	6	—2	7.3
1956–55	4	3	3	0	4	11	1	5	—9	2	4	—6	2.0
1957–56	7	—2	9	—3	2	8	8	6	2	0	2	—6	3.6
1958–57	6	11	9	—13	13	12	8	8	18	10	2	—1	7.9
1959–58	17	16	25	15	10	22	13	21	24	7	73	31	17.3
Geometric Mean	6.5	10.6	11.9	3.3	10.3	14.1	11.2	10.9	10.7	9.6	11.8	6.3	10.4

introduction to this chapter, there is no doubt that the market expects to find some constancy in the results of firms, even if only of an extremely weak kind. Just to mention some favourite growth shares, such as London Brick, Longmans Green, or Marks and Spencer, may seem almost sufficient in itself to prove a rule that some firms rather consistently do better for the investor than the average. Part of this consistency might result from the market deciding that the firm was going to do well, and thus forcing the price up to prove itself correct. However, this could not continue for long without similar earnings growth, and therefore it seems certain that there must be some consistency in earnings corresponding to that observed in prices. But this really proves nothing, because, even if growth was quite independent of past performance, we would expect some companies to do better than the average simply as a result of chance factors. This would be no indication that they would continue to prosper in the future. Admittedly, the longer that any growth stock continues to grow faster than the average, the less likely it is that this can be the result of chance alone. Nevertheless, it is on the cards that a few companies will do so for many years.

Therefore, before attempting to make any statistical analysis of growth, we shall simply plot for two industries the actual growth paths; this should convince the reader that there is at least no simple and obvious division into successful and unsuccessful firms. The two industries chosen are stores and building (since the first has been one of the favourite industries, and the second is analyzed at some length later in the chapter). The results are shown on Charts 1.1 and 1.2, where the percentage growth in pre-tax earnings, expressed as the difference from the industry average for the same year, are plotted against time. In each case the 'favourite son' of the market (barred line) is plotted with a randomly selected group of five other firms. Even with this small number the results are somewhat confused, giving the impression of a drawn-out twisted cobweb.

If there is some really steady pattern of growth, we would expect to find the firms remaining at more or less the same distance above or below the zero (average) line. This is hardly the case. If some random variation is added to this constant behaviour, then we would expect fluctuations, but still leaving some residual trend line above or below the centre. In this case, it is possible to say

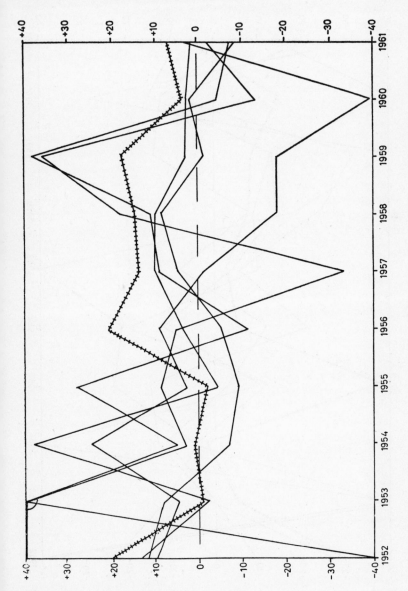

Chart 1.1. The percentage growth of earnings pre-tax plotted as the difference from the industry percentage growth for the same year for various stores.

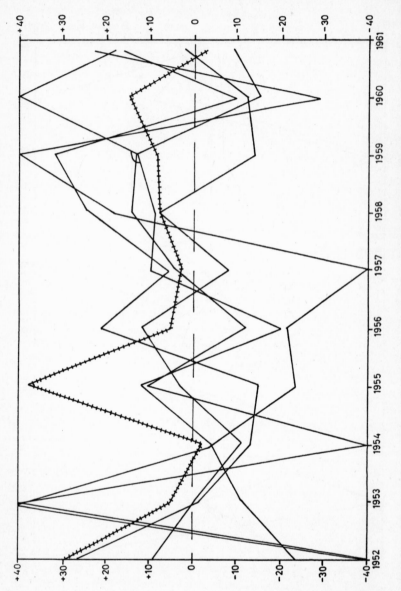

Chart 1.2. The percentage growth of earnings pre-tax plotted as the difference from the industry percentage growth for the same year for various building firms.

that the 'favourite sons' do fit in with this theory. They are shown by the barred time paths, and are Marks and Spencer, and Rugby Portland Cement. These were chosen because they were the firms in the two industries from which the market demanded the lowest yield over the period. Particularly in the case of Marks and Spencer there seems to be some visible trend with variations about the +10 per cent level. Unfortunately, the other firms do not show any such consistency, but seem to wander all over the charts without any reference to their past behaviour. One can perhaps see some short run trends in some of the firms, but not many, and this is contrasted to the strange habit of other firms of always reversing their movement of the previous year. But again, this is by no means always the case. In short, it would be difficult to convince oneself that the performance of the firms that do show some consistent growth is any more than the result of chance factors.

In fact, it is rather optimistic to think that it would be possible to see some clear pattern emerging from plotting these graphs on this simple annual basis. There are three main reasons for this:

1. We can expect that there will be large random factors affecting the profits of a firm, which will be beyond the control of the management; therefore, there are likely to be fluctuations in the earnings path which will tend to cover any trend that there might be. This is more likely to be the case in an industry whose total sales fluctuate to a large extent over time, and therefore should affect investment industries more than consumption or service industries. This is perhaps borne out by the fact that there appear to be more fluctuation in the chart for the building industry than in the one for stores;[1] however, the charts show too small a sample of firms to be able to come to any definite conclusion. This first reason should not bias any attempt to find any relationship in growth over time, but it will make the relationship less exact.

2. The second reason is of vital importance for the rest of the chapter. It is that a random increase or decrease in earnings (that is, one that occurs beyond the control of the managers), will both increase earnings growth in the current year,

---

[1] Building contractors were deliberately excluded, so the fact that their earnings often fluctuate markedly, because of the timing of bringing profits on large contracts into the accounts, is not an explanation.

and decrease it in the following one, and vice versa. This will lead to a negative bias when considering the relation between the growth of one year and the next, since growth will tend to be followed by decline, independent of any activity on the part of the management. This will be a serious nuisance later in our statistical analysis, as can be foreseen by observing how often the time paths on the two charts follow a zig-zag pattern.

3. The third reason which helps to obliterate any pattern on these charts is that of the reversibility and size of change. A fall of earnings to a low level requires only a very small absolute improvement in the following year for the growth rate to be enormous. Thus any considerable fall in earnings is likely to be followed by an apparently vast rise, since we are using percentage growth figures. This point will be considered in a later part of this chapter; but it is worth pointing out here, while we are observing these charts, that the use of percentage changes causes violent behaviour in the earnings path after it falls to any very low figure.

One hope left, in using charts to see growth patterns, is to aggregate firms together in some way, and then look at the growth path of the group of firms. If one is lucky, most of the random fluctuations will be cancelled out inside the group, leaving just the trend to be observed. The most reasonable method of grouping these firms is according to rate of growth, so that we can see whether the fastest growing group, for example, continues to grow faster than the rest. Therefore the large firms were divided into ten groups according to their speed of growth during some period of time, and then the path of the future average growth in the group was plotted. For this section, and all subsequent ones, the maximum rate of growth was placed at 100 per cent so as to decrease the problem of size of change mentioned in Point 3 above. The sample of large firms used was those with complete financial records from 1951 to 1959, in number 441.

In Charts 1.3, 1.4, and 1.5, the period used to select the groupings for speed of growth was four years. On the basis of the growth in this period, the firms were divided, irrespective of industry, into ten groups: the fastest growing tenth of the firms, the second fastest, etc. The periods used were: 1951–1955 in Chart 1.3, 1952–1956 in Chart 1.4, and 1953–1957 in Chart 1.5. In Chart 1.6 the period used to divide according to growth was six years, from 1951–

1957. In all four cases, the first year of the growth testing period was used as a base of 100 from which to compare later performance. The arithmetic mean growth rate for each set was then calculated, and plotted as a deviation from the arithmetic mean growth rate of the whole sample, on semi-log paper, together with the subsequent performance of the ten sets of firms (also taken as deviations from the mean of all firms). The subsequent dividend performance was also plotted as well as the subsequent pre-tax earnings. There is, as stated earlier, reason to expect that dividends will show a more stable relationship over time than earnings, since, in the short run, directors can influence the dividend rate independently of what is happening to earnings.

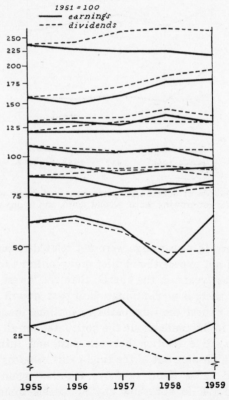

Chart 1.3. Indices of subsequent performance of mean earnings and dividends of the fastest growing tenth, second tenth, and so on, of large firms in the period 1951–55.

C

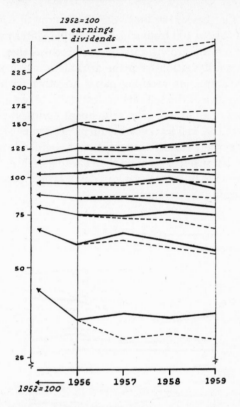

Chart 1.4. Indices of subsequent performance of mean earnings and dividends of the fastest growing tenth, second tenth, and so on, of large firms in the period 1952–56.

If future growth of earnings were not related to past growth, then we would not expect the highest group of firms to grow any faster, in the last years on the charts, than the lowest group. In other words, if there is no continuation of past growth behaviour, then we would expect the time paths to continue in a horizontal line, or rather to fluctuate about the horizontal, for all the groups of firms. A positive relation between past and future growth should lead to a fanning out of the time paths, whereas a negative relation should cause them to move together again. In fact, Charts 1.3 and 1.4 do not show any noticeable trend from the horizontal for earnings in the years after the first four, apart perhaps from a weak suggestion of a reversal of the growth; and,

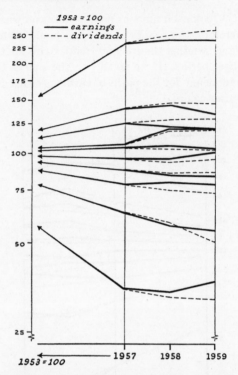

Chart 1.5. Indices of subsequent performance of mean earnings and dividends of the fastest growing tenth, second tenth, and so on, of large firms in the period 1953–57.

therefore, again show no convincing relation over time. Charts 1.5 and 1.6 do appear to show some continuation of growth pattern for one year, but after this there does not seem to be any further continuation. However, neither of these weak suggestions of continuation or reversal for one year must be taken too seriously. Since the figures plotted are deviations from the overall average, this means that approximately five of the earnings' paths must rise, and five fall each year. If we ignore the possibility of horizontal paths, then there must be, even on the most even distribution, three of the five above the 100 line rising (or falling) and three falling (or rising) below it. Even this will look like a trend toward continuation or reversal of the previous pattern. Moreover, it is not likely that such an even pattern will happen very often by chance, and any deviation from it will make the resultant paths look even more as if they were conforming to some pattern. Therefore, the results of one year alone cannot be much help in telling us whether there is any trend; to decide this we must observe a longer period. If we do this on the charts, then there is no apparent tendency for the paths of earnings either to fan out or to come together again.

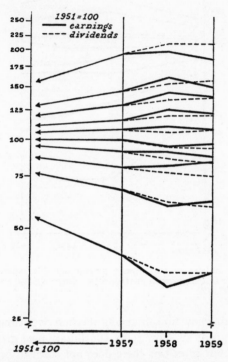

Chart 1.6. Indices of subsequent performance of mean earnings and dividends of the fastest growing tenth, second tenth, and so on, of large firms in the period 1951–57.

The case of dividends is quite different, however. Here there is clearly in each chart (though not quite so clear in 1.3 as in the others) a tendency for the dividend paths to fan out, continuing the shape of the growth of earnings in the earlier period. This suggests that the growth is correlated to past earnings growth, and probably also to past dividend growth. (This latter is not certain since the growth rates of the firms are ranked on past earnings rather than dividend records.)

Two further comments on these charts suggest themselves. First, there appears to be a tendency for the lowest two groups to exhibit larger fluctuations in their paths than the others. This is presumably the result of the fact, mentioned above, that a large fall in earnings or dividends allows a very large increase in the percentage growth figure, even if there is not a large absolute growth. Apart from these two groups, the large fluctuations from year to year have, as expected, been cancelled out in the process of aggregation. Secondly, if there is an appearance of a continuing pattern of growth, as in the case of dividends, this could be merely the result of differences between industries, rather than firms. Thus, if there are several firms in the top group belonging to the fastest growing industry, then if this group continues to grow faster, or if its dividends continue to grow faster, the reason may be that it is the industry that is continuing to grow faster than

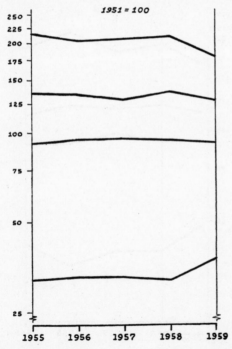

Chart 1.7. Indices of subsequent growth of mean earnings of the fastest growing quartile, second quartile, and so on, of small firms in the period 1951–55.

other industries. Inside the industry, there may be no similar patterns in the growth of the firms relative to the industry average. This introduces the concept of 'between industry relations' and 'within industry relations'. We are primarily interested in the latter. Since the management of one company can have little effect on the prosperity of the whole industry, all it can do is to manoeuvre within the industry. Moreover, so far as the investor is concerned, he must choose between industries on quite different grounds from his choice between firms in an industry. He should predict the future of the industry separately from his belief in the continuing relative growth patterns of the constituent firms of the industry. Therefore, we shall in future attempt to distinguish between these two parts of firms' growth, and will concentrate on the within industry relation. But, in the case of the above charts,

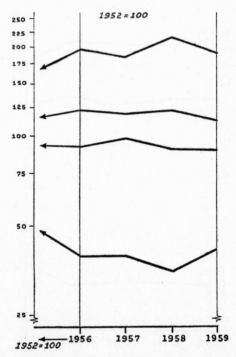

Chart 1.8. Indices of subsequent growth of mean earnings of the fastest growing quartile, second quartile, and so on, of small firms in the period 1952–56.

the dividend pattern would appear to be too clear to be caused by this spurious 'between industry' growth pattern, since such a hypothesis would imply a remarkably strong, clear-cut, distinction between the growth of different industries.

The sample of small firms has also been dealt with in the same way in Charts 1.7, 1.8, 1.9 and 1.10. The only differences from the earlier ones are that the firms were divided into four groups, instead of ten, because of the smaller number in the sample; and that dividends are not plotted. Here the same comments that were made about the previous charts can be repeated again. There appears to be the same tendency for growth to be reversed in the first charts (1.7, 1.8) for one year only, and then to remain moving around the same level; and in the latter two (1.9, 1.10) the trend seems to continue for one year, and then be reversed. However, since there are only four groups this

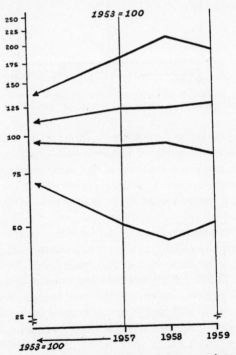

Chart 1.9. Indices of subsequent growth of mean earnings of the fastest growing quartile, second quartile, and so on, of small firms in the period 1953–57.

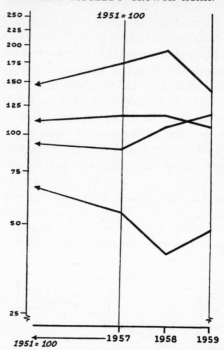

Chart 1.10. Indices of subsequent growth of mean earnings of the fastest growing quartile, second quartile, and so on, of small firms in the period 1951–57.

time, it is even more dangerous to attempt to draw any clear conclusion from the paths of just one year. In fact, it is rather unlikely that random variations of the firms' earnings would *not* give rise to some apparent 'pattern' for one year; the lack of any pattern over a longer period again suggests that there is no such real pattern.

The only conclusion we can draw from this section on charting growth, is that any relation over time of earnings change is too well hidden for it to be discovered at this crude level. Working within an industry, individual fluctuations are too strong to be able to observe any pattern, except in the one or two firms that we already knew to do well, and even this may be the result of chance. At the aggregate level, we have lost the fluctuations, but we have also lost any relationship that might have existed before we aggregated. Therefore, we require another approach that will allow us to find out what happens on the average amongst the firms in an industry; and which can allow for the large fluctuations resulting from random factors, and still find if there is any relation underlying them.

Statistical analysis might be able to do this—at least it can tell us with more certainty what is the likelihood of there being some relationship over time. It is designed to take note of the random fluctuations, and then state how probable it is that any apparent pattern under the fluctuations could arise through chance factors alone. However, since its methods are rigid, it is also problematic in application, and may well give misleading results, in that it cannot take note of biases that might occur because of some unexpected spurious connection between the figures over time—the person using the statistical methods must make some attempt to find these biases himself. As we shall see in this chapter, and in the following one, this question of bias is vital in this analysis, and it is by no means clear that we have discovered all the biases entering into these investigations. This statistical consideration of growth has been done in three different ways, starting from the least sophisticated, and moving to a slightly higher level; albeit still using techniques that are far from the *dernier cri* in statistical detection. Rather than describe these methods here, we shall introduce them as the reasons for their use become apparent.

The first attempt uses a series of differing approaches to the pre-tax earnings record of the 33 firms in the building industry that had continuous records from 1951 to 1961. Only one industry was analysed, since it was a preliminary investigation to try varying methods to see if it were possible to obtain any significant results with them; the fact that they were not extended to cover the whole sample of firms is a correct indication that the results were not very convincing. However, since this will be the case for the whole chapter, it is still worth demonstrating these inconclusive results.

Two series of figures were used in this section:—

1. The annual percentage growth in earnings of each company for each year, with the limitation that a figure of 75 per cent was the largest value for this growth. This arbitrary limit was imposed in order to lessen the effect of very considerable growth and decline following relatively small changes in actual earnings. It was used 17 times out of a total of 330 observations.

2. The change in earnings expressed as a percentage of the average earnings for the company over the period of eleven years.

In both cases there were observations for each company for the last ten years of the period, since there could be no observation for the first year because there were no figures for the preceding year. In both cases the growth figure was sometimes expressed as the deviation from the industry average growth in the same year.

It is difficult to know what are theoretically the correct figures to use when measuring earnings growth. It is possible to stand back from this, and say that growth *means* annual percentage change, and that these are the figures to examine for consistency. However, if one approaches the problem from the management's viewpoint, then it is necessary to think in terms of a planning period. If this is, say, three to five years, then it is weighting the dice against consistency to use a shorter period to measure growth. Growth must mean growth from something, and this should be the earnings expected by the management rather than from something that has occurred partly by chance. If the planning horizon is about four years, then it would be best to take the average earnings for the same period as the measure of capacity from which growth is taken. This would imply the use of a moving average of earnings from which to measure growth. Unfortunately, our series of observations is too short to use any form of moving average, and therefore the only real way to use this idea of a measure of capacity from which to measure growth is to use the average earnings over the whole period as the base (as in series 2). From the point of view of the planning horizon, this is too long; while series 1 is too short.

All this is saying no more than that, since the planning period is generally longer than one year, we must expect large annual fluctuations if we use simple annual ·percentage growth figures. The use of some longer period as a base to measure capacity will not remove these annual fluctuations, but it will mean that each fluctuation is nearer the true value for the year rather than a variation from the previous partly random fluctuation, i.e., it will show up more of the true growth for *that* year.

The question of whether it is correct to deflate the change in earnings by anything, whether instead the figure considered should be the absolute change in earnings, will be considered in a later section. One advantage that the second series does have, is that it avoids the problem resulting from low levels of earnings causing vast annual growth with only a small absolute increase. But unfortunately, the problem of a large fall in earnings is worsened, since it becomes possible for a fall to be more than 100 per cent. Nevertheless, the total number of changes larger than 75 per cent is only six in series 2.

The first use of these two series merely considers the direction of the change in earnings expressed as a deviation from the industry average. In other words, it simply considers whether or not there was any consistency in terms of firms' behaviour compared with the average. Were there firms which continually did better than the average, and therefore had positive signs attached to their growth expressed as a deviation from the average? The actual frequency distribution of positive signs, showing the number of years that the firm beat the industry, is shown below in Table 1.5. (Zeros were alternately considered positive and negative.)

TABLE 1.5

The number of firms in the building industry that exceed the average rate of earnings growth for differing numbers of years

No. of years in which average was exceeded.

	0	1	2	3	4	5	6	7	8	9	10
Earnings growth measured by series 1	0	0	1	5	11	8	4	3	1	0	0
Earnings growth measured by series 2	0	0	1	3	8	10	5	3	2	1	0
Theoretical Binomial distribution	.03	.32	1.45	3.87	6.77	8.12	6.77	3.87	1.45	.32	.03

NOTE.—Since these figures are concerned only with the sign of the deviations, they need not average exactly about the mean of 5 years, as would be the case if we were considering the actual size of the deviations. The fact that series 1 appears to have a negative bias probably results from the fact that there were a number of very large positive changes as discussed above. In the case of series 2 this bias has, as expected, virtually disappeared.

The distribution of the number of successful years, as shown in Table 1.5, does not directly tell us whether it is possible to separate the firms into the ones that consistently do well, and those that consistently do badly; though there is some concentration about the central figures, suggesting that most firms vary between success and failure. In fact, the 'favourite son', Rugby Portland

Cement, is the company that does best in both series, collecting eight successes in the first, and nine in the second. But, is it anything other than the firm that does best as a result of purely chance factors? (Our apologies to Sir Halford Reddish!)

If one likens this problem to one of tossing a coin, then if we were repeatedly to toss it ten times, we should expect that on many occasions we would get more or less than exactly five heads, though this would be the average number we would expect. If we assume that the sign of the deviation in any one year has no relation to the sign in previous years, then the problem in the case of growth is the same as that of tossing a coin, apart from the small bias that makes the average, in the case of series 1, 4.67 positive signs instead of exactly five. This bias is small enough not to have any significant effect on the results. Tossing a coin results in the number of heads being distributed according to the binomial distribution, and we can use this distribution to calculate the distribution of positive signs we should expect in this case. This is shown in the bottom line of Table 1.5. As can be seen, the actual distribution does not differ very much from this, and using the Chi squared test to see whether the actual figures differ significantly (i.e. in some way unlikely to happen by chance alone) from this theoretical distribution, we find that we cannot dismiss the likelihood that the figures are generated by some such process as in the binomial distribution. (In fact the Chi squared values are 4.28 and 1.62, splitting the distribution into five sections, whereas Chi at the 5 per cent level is 9.49 for four degrees of freedom.)

The implication of this is that even if there is no relation between the present success of the firm and its past success or failure, then it is still very possible for the observed distribution of successes to arise. Therefore, Rugby Portland Cement may just happen to be the firm that has done best by chance: it may be no more likely to continue to succeed than it is to throw a further head after having thrown nine in ten attempts.

However, this is rather a crude attempt to find any pattern in growth over time, since it ignores both the size of the changes and the pattern over the period of ten years. It considers only how many times the firm has beaten the industry; not differentiating between five successes followed by five failures, and a random distribution of the two. Therefore, there is still some possibility that a relationship may be found when we also consider the size and pattern of deviations.

The earlier sections in this chapter mentioned the possibility of bias, caused by some factor beyond the management's control, affecting earnings in one year; and thus causing growth to move in opposite directions for that year and the next . In other words, a windfall gain makes the current year's growth look better, but will make next year appear to be worse, unless some similar windfall reoccurs. This bias will have to be considered at all stages in this chapter. In the present example, it would have the effect of making the distribution of successes more concentrated at the centre. Thus, a firm that is rising steadily with no random variation would show a series of positive deviations from the average. If there were random elements added, but with no pattern over time, then the series of positive signs would not be so consistent; this randomness is directly allowed for in the Chi squared test. However, with the fluctuations being tied together in the negative way explained above, there will be a stronger tendency for the firm to have a more equal number of positive and negative signs than the Chi squared test allows for. Therefore, this bias makes the test of less validity, though whether it is sufficient to reverse the result found, cannot be said directly.

In an attempt to see how important this bias was, the same two series were observed to see what was the relationship over time for success and failure in pairs of years. For each two years there are four possibilities—a positive deviation could be followed by either a negative or a positive, and similarly when the first deviation is negative. Therefore, out of the four cases, two would have deviations of the same sign and two different. If there were no bias, or trend relation over time, then we would expect that these two alternatives would have equal probability. But a bias would lead to a preponderance of different signs as explained above; whereas, if there were some trend of past growth leading to further growth, then we would expect the majority of cases to have the same signs.

For each firm, there are nine pairs of years adjoining each other, and so with 33 firms we have a total of 297 observations. Of these the number with similar signs were 152 in the case of series 1, and 159 in the case of series 2. The remainders (145 and 138) were of different sign. It can be easily seen that this is very close to an even distribution, and in fact the Chi squared test again demonstrated that it was not nearly significantly different from such an even distribution. This implies either that there is no bias nor any constancy of growth in the short run; or else that both are present, but since they work in opposite directions, have cancelled each other out. This confirms the findings of the similar test above, and so leaves us again with no firm conclusion as to whether there is bias or trend. The only hint given is that since we can be certain that there is some bias from theoretical grounds, though it may be very weak, therefore there is an implication that there must be some tendency towards a constancy of growth over time, though this also may be extremely weak.

The investigation of the building industry was concluded by the application of the technique of analysis of variance to the growth figures 1 and 2. This technique looks at the variation in the growth figures, and shows whether there is a significant part of this variation that can be explained by the division of the figures into company, or year, groups. If this division does significantly reduce the variation, then we can say that the difference between companies or years is of importance; if it does not, then again it would appear that firms are not really different from each other, and that therefore the management is not of importance in distinguishing them apart, and that business cycles were not significant in affecting the performance of the companies during the period.

The figures in series 1 were analysed by this method as actual growth figures, rather than as deviations from the industry average. The results are shown in Table 1.6 below.

TABLE 1.6

Analysis of variance of yearly growth in the building industry

	Degrees of Freedom	Sums of Squares	Variance Estimate	F Ratio
Between companies	32	13,131	410	.49
Between years	9	15,081	1,676	2.01
Residual	288	239,815	832	
Total	329	268,027		

The F ratios, at the 5 per cent level, as calculated in statistical tables are as follows:

$$F_{30/200}=1.52 \qquad F_{9/200}=1.92$$

This result shows the difference between years to be significant at the 5 per cent level, though only just, but the difference between firms seems far from any sign of significance. The same was the case with the series 2 figures, though here the deviations from the industry average for each year were used, and so there was no concept of a 'between years' component of the variance. The 'between firm' F ratio was 0.79, again insignificant.

Both these results suggest once more that there is no consistent pattern of growth that distinguishes one firm from another.[1] Before evaluating the importance of this conclusion, there are two comments to be made on the question of bias as it effects this last analysis. First, the year to year effect, mentioned above, should have little direct effect on significance, since it will increase the variance for all firms. Analysis of variance takes no note of the sign of deviations (which is one fault in its use in this problem,

[1] It is worth comparing these results with the seemingly opposite ones found by Professor Barna in his pamphlet *Investment and Growth Policies in British Industrial Firms*. (Cambridge University Press, 1962). The parts that concern us here are Chapter Two, and Appendix C which gives the statistical proof for the chapter in the form of similar analysis of variance tables to the one shown above.

Barna was concerned with the growth and profits of firms in the food processing and electrical engineering industries between 1949 and mid-1959. His measures of growth were the gross increase in fixed (or total) assets during the year as a percentage of the gross value of fixed (or total) assets at the beginning of the year. Profit rates were measured as the ratio of profits before deducting depreciation, taxation, and long term interest, but after deducting bank interest, to a corresponding definition of total assets.

He did an analysis of variance on the growth rate figures (p. 70), dividing the variation between firms and between years, and in the food industry also between trades and between size groups. His results are stated on page 10 as follows: 'The conclusion is that differences between firms in rates of growth are large and that only a small part of these differences could be attributed to size or to the trade in which the firm operates; most of the differences are differences between firms in comparable situations. . . .'

'On any of the usual statistical tests the differences between firms in average growth rates calculated for a period of nine years are significant and these differences between individual firms outweigh in importance differences from one year to another. The rate of growth thus appears to characterize the individual firm rather than the industry or trade, the size of the firm, or particular years.'

But Professor Barna's measure of growth is so fundamentally different from ours that no comparison can really be drawn. An increase in assets is very different from an increase in earnings per share, adjusted for capital changes. A company which grows rapidly in asset size, may have no increase in earnings per share. It can grow by borrowing, or by buying other companies for an issue of shares. There have in fact been many growth companies in Barna's sense, which are by no means growth companies in our sense. No more need be said, so far as growth rates are concerned.

Turning to profit rates, Barna did a similar analysis, and came up with similar results: 'The statistical tests have shown that differences between average profitability for individual firms were highly significant in relation to changes in profitability from year to year for the same firm' (p. 12). Does this conflict with our results? Professor Barna was concerned with average profitability, and we with changes in earnings per share. The latter are not the same

where direction is of considerable importance): it merely considers whether any trend occurring beneath the fluctuations is of sufficient importance to say that it significantly distinguishes between the firms; On the other hand, in that the fluctuations do increase the total variance, it becomes more difficult for the difference between firms to be significant. Secondly, the mean growth rate for each firm over ten years plays an integral part in the calculation of the between firm variance. Now, this mean rate depends on the earnings figures for the first and last years of the period, and, therefore, any unusual factor affecting one of these years will

---

thing as changes in profitability on Barna's definition. Some differences could certainly result from this. On the other hand, our concept is likely to be closely releated to Barna's, and so no dramatic difference in our conclusions should result. So let us first pretend, for the sake of argument, that we were measuring differences in profitability as defined by Barna.

In that case, the difference between the analysis of profits boils down to the fact that we were concerned to see if there was any significant difference between firms in the growth of profit rate, and could not find it, while Barna looked for, and found, a difference in the average level of the profit rate. These two are quite compatible. Thus a random-walk pattern of growth of profit rates (which would fit our results quite closely) will lead to statistically significant differences in average profit rates. Or, in other words, if the growth in the profit rate has no relation to the previous year's growth, we would still expect the average profit rate to show some relation to the previous year's figures, since the growth in the rate has been from the previous year's level. Thus, if the growth has an equal chance to be up or down from the previous year's level, then we would expect on average that the level for the next year would be the same as that for the previous year, i.e. there would be some average relation.

The question is whether we should look at year to year changes, or long period averages, in deciding whether there is any significant difference between firms. Though we have tended to use the short period changes, Barna can use long period averages provided it is realized that the differences he comes across can be the result of purely random growth of profit rates from year to year, rather than a result of long term planning on the part of management. Consequently, statistically significant differences in average profit rates cannot in themselves be taken as signs of differences in management.

But there is still one puzzling point. Within some particular industry, consider a set of firms with high profit rates, which, according to the random-walk hypothesis, have come about by chance. Now if their rate of profit on money ploughed back is randomly distributed about this high level, as the random walk theory would suggest, the mean rate of profit on such money would be above the industry mean. To this extent their earnings growth rate should also be greater than the industry average, which would be contrary to our findings. But this possible inconsistency need not worry us much, since money ploughed back at different profit rates could not account for much of any divergence of growth between different sets of companies. The 'bias' operating in favour of the more profitable companies would be very slight (indeed, in Section (5) of this Chapter, we fail to detect any influence of the amount ploughed back, on growth). It must also be recalled that our hypothesis is of randomness in the growth of adjusted earnings per share, not of randomness in the growth of profitability on assets. Although, as we have said, this should lead to no dramatic difference between our results and those of Barna, it might well upset as fine a point as the present one.

affect the average growth over the whole period. This effect, which will be considered again later, implies that there would be a tendency to exaggerate the difference between firms rather than to diminish it. Therefore, even if the results were significant, we would have some reason to doubt them.

The analysis of variance would seem to cast even more of a doubt on the possibility of any pattern of earnings growth over time; but there are still several flaws in this approach. One is the point, mentioned in the previous paragraph, that it does not take account of the sign of the deviations; this can be extended to say that the method fails to take note of any pattern in the deviations, merely considering the average growth as compared to the fluctuations. This pattern of deviations may be of considerable importance in deciding whether there is some real pattern of growth; however, when this result is observed in conjunction with the previous findings on signs, which looked at patterns rather than size, then the picture is not too hopeful for finding some significant result.

However, we have yet to consider the pattern and size of these movements at the same time, and also to consider other industries, so there may still be some possibility of success. The next step in the search for some relationship moves to the use of correlation methods. Here, the whole sample of larger companies was used, plus a few that did not have complete records, since it was possible to include these for some of the short period correlations. For these firms, annual compound growth rates were calculated for every period 1951–1952, 1951–1953 and so on up to 1951–1959; also 1952–1953, 1952–1954, up to 1952–1959; also for 1953–1954, and so on. As in the case of the charts, the maximum growth in any period was limited to 100 per cent.

Correlation coefficients were then calculated for each industry group (mechanical engineering continuing to be divided into two sections) as follows. First, the growth in earnings for one year was correlated with the growth in the previous year—earnings growth 52/53 correlated with growth for 51/52, then 53/54 with 52/53, up to 58/59 correlated with 57/58: a total of seven correlations for each group. Next, the growth in one year was correlated with the growth in the previous two years—53/54 with 51/53, up to 58/59 correlated with 56/58: a total of six correlations for each group. Thirdly, growth of earnings in one year was correlated with growth in the previous three years, giving five correlations

D

for each group; then, similarly, growth in one year with the previous four, five, six, and seven years. After this, growth for two years was correlated with the growth for the previous two ,three, four, five, and six years, in the same way. This was continued until the growth for four years was correlated with the growth for the first four years of the time period. The results are shown in Table 1.7, for the first eight industry groups giving the sign and average value for the correlation coefficients calculated.[1]

The calculations were done for the industry groups, rather than by simply lumping all firms together, since, as before, it was thought that the management should be considered in its performance relative to the rest of the firms in the same industry, and the inter-industry effect should therefore be avoided.

TABLE 1.7
Unlagged Correlations of Growth on Growth—Large Companies

No. of Years in Earlier Period	No. of Years in Later Period	No. of Correlations	No. Positive	No. Negative	Mean
1	1	55	19	36	−.11
2	1	47	14	33	−.18
3	1	39	8	31	−.17
4	1	31	6	25	−.11
5	1	23	9	14	−.06
6	1	15	5	10	.05
7	1	8	1	7	−.15
8	1	1	0	1	−.31
2	2	40	7	33	−.22
3	2	33	10	23	−.14
4	2	24	14	10	−.05
5	2	16	10	6	−.05
6	2	9	3	6	−.08
7	2	1	0	1	−.59
3	3	24	8	16	−.06
4	3	16	7	9	.00
5	3	9	5	4	−.01
6	3	1	0	1	−.42
4	4	9	5	4	.02
5	4	1	0	1	−.37
TOTALS		402	131	271	−.12

Note.—The sample size of the above results varied from 22 to 55 with a mean of 39.

From an inspection of Table 1.7, it can easily be seen that both the numbers and the mean value show a preponderance of negative values for the correlation coefficients, whereas, if there was some

[1] The numbers of correlations shown in the tables do not follow exactly from this explanation, since 1960 results were available for one group; and there were some other complications.

TABLE 1.8
Lagged Correlations of Growth on Growth—Large Companies

No. of Years in Earlier Period	No. of Years in Later Period	No. of Correlations	No. Positive	No. Negative	Mean
1	1	47	11	36	−.13
2	1	39	13	26	−.11
3	1	31	13	18	−.05
4	1	23	14	9	−.02
5	1	15	8	7	−.12
6	1	8	3	5	.10
7	1	1	0	1	−.34
2	2	33	12	21	−.06
3	2	24	13	11	.00
4	2	16	10	6	.02
5	2	9	4	5	.00
6	2	1	0	1	−.43
3	3	16	10	6	.09
4	3	9	5	4	.08
5	3	1	0	1	−.28
4	4	1	0	1	−.31
TOTALS		274	116	158	−.05

relation of growth leading to future growth, one would expect the positive coefficients to outnumber the negative ones. However, we have now met the idea of a bias affecting the results a sufficient number of times to suspect that it might be operating yet again. Indeed, this must be the case, since in every one of the correlations, what was being done was to relate two growth figures, one from a given year into the future for a period, and the other from some time in the past to the same year, i.e.

$$\frac{\text{Earnings in the given year}}{\text{Earnings } x \text{ years ago}}\text{was correlated with}$$

$$\frac{\text{Earnings in } y \text{ years time}}{\text{Earnings in the given year}}, \text{ where } x \text{ is the period of growth in the}$$

past and y is the period in the future. These ratios are then turned into the annual compound growth rates used in the analysis. Thus with four years in the earlier period, and three in the later period, what is being calculated is the relation between

$$\frac{\text{Earnings 1955}}{\text{Earnings 1951}} \text{ and } \frac{\text{Earnings 1958}}{\text{Earnings 1955}}. \text{ Whatever the period, there}$$

will always be the same figure for earnings in the numerator of the first growth ratio, and in the denominator of the second.

Therefore, any random factor beyond the control of the management will increase one of these ratios, and decrease the other, leading to a negative relation between the two, other things being equal. If we think that there are factors which have important effects on the earnings of companies, and which are not controlled by the management, and are therefore outside the relationship we expect to find, then we must expect a negative bias in our results, which will have similar effects on every period of growth considered, but with the bias being less strong in the longer ones.

For the longer periods, the fact that the growth figures have to be turned into compound growth rates slightly complicates the picture, but leaves basically the same bias. In fact, the pattern of the bias should be more or less as follows: if we assume that the random element is a proportionate increase or decrease in earnings, then, whether this is at the beginning or end of a period, its effect will decrease the longer is the period. In other words, over a long period, the variation in the first or last year due to random elements will only have a small effect on the average growth rate of the period. This implies that in these results the bias will decrease with (1) a constant first period and an increasing second period, and (2) an increasing first period and a constant second period. It is just about possible to convince oneself that these considerations are realized in Table 1.7. However, to see it, it is necessary to discount the four correlations for the longest period which have only one observation each, and therefore are not of any significance when compared with the whole table. In both tables 1.7 and 1.8 these longest period correlations involve the same group, which seems rather to disagree with the trends in all the other groups. It was the only one for which 1960 results were available when the original article was being written.

This can explain why there is such a negative tendency in the table of correlation coefficients for the first eight groups, but it cannot tell us whether this bias was swamping some positive relationship hidden underneath it. In order to reduce the effect of the bias, the same eight industry groups were recalculated, but with a lag between the growth ratios, so that the two periods did not overlap. Thus for the correlations of one year and one year, 1954–53 was related to 1952–51, and 1955–54 to 1953–52, etc., while for periods of two and two years, 1956–54 was related to

1953–51, and 1957–55 to 1954–52, etc. This reduced the number of correlations for each of the time periods. The results are presented in Table 1.8, where it can be seen that the bias is reduced. But there is still a definite tendency towards a negative value, though if the four longest correlations (with the total number of years in both periods equal to eight) are removed from the table, the results look better, particularly for the longer periods. Before coming to any conclusion about these results, it would be as well to see what has happened to the bias.

We are now correlating $\dfrac{\text{Earnings in the previous year}}{\text{Earnings } x+1 \text{ years ago}}$ with

$\dfrac{\text{Earnings in } y \text{ years time}}{\text{Earnings in the given year}}$, with the periods as before, and

with the conversion of these figures into annual growth rates also as before. Has this removed the problem of bias? Presumably only partially, since it would be too much to expect these random variations in earnings to remain conveniently within the financial year. Therefore, there will be certainly some increases or decreases which will occur during the period that includes both the end of the previous year and the beginning of the given year. A windfall sales contract, or a strike, will effect the earnings for a period of a few months which may well be in both financial years. Certainly, the bias will be much reduced, but it is not likely to be eliminated.

In Table 1.8 the pattern of bias caused by the turning of the earnings ratios into growth figures can be observed, but this time it is much more clear. If one discounts the four long-period correlations with large negative signs, and also allows for the bias particularly affecting the first, second, and eighth, rows of the table, then one is left with an even distribution between positive and negative values for the correlation coefficients. But these rather tenuous reasons for carefully selecting the rows to concentrate on, must throw some doubt on the meaning of the final result.

As a further demonstration of the inconclusiveness of the results, and of evidence of bias, Chart 1.11 shows the distribution of the 55 calculated unlagged, and the 47 calculated lagged, correlation coefficients of one year on one year's growth. The slight negative mean and skewness of the unlagged results is apparent. The negative tendency of the lagged results is rather less, but still visible.

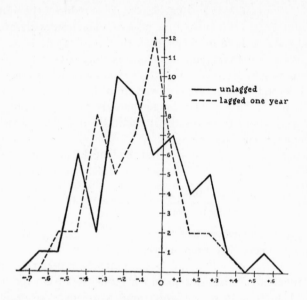

Chart 1.11. Distribution of correlation coefficients of One Year's growth with another.

Moreover, there are still two further causes for objection to this method of analysis. The first is that in calculating growth rates, only the first and last figures for earnings had any effect on the actual rate as noted earlier. The implication of this is that over a long period, whatever happens to the firm in the years in the middle of the period is irrelevant to the growth trend (if there is a trend). If there is little variation from year to year in the growth pattern, then this is a reasonable implication. However, we do know that there is considerable variation, so that the figure calculated for the growth rate will frequently be quite atypical of the actual performance of a company over the longer periods. The effect of this will be to lessen any relationship that might exist over time in that we will find it harder to observe it using this method; but it should not lead to a bias in the results.

The second objection is rather similar, which is that the technique of calculating correlation coefficients gives considerably greater weight to figures that are a long way from the average for the whole group. Therefore atypical results caused by factors such as the one above, or by the problem of the artificial valuation of growth for cases where earnings are at very low levels, or simply by some real large change in the firm's earnings, will make the correlation coefficient as calculated not really representative of the whole industry.

Considering these two points, and the question of bias, it must be admitted that some doubt attaches to the correlation analysis of the original article as a means of discovering whether companies have trend rates of growth which differ. Not too surprisingly, the results for mechanical engineering (31st December) were as inconclusive as the rest, even though one had hoped to find some more significant results in this case.

Though this bias does rather invalidate the original correlation analysis, two points should be noted: first, that at the time of writing the original article, very few people would have thought that there could be such a large bias affecting the year to year growth figures: secondly, that this bias is in fact a real world phenomenon, and is not merely a statistical problem. It is real in the sense that it may impoverish a naïve investor who has no evidence other than a fairly short period of high growth, and who sells when results disappoint (provided there are enough such naïve investors to force up the price unduly on a good chancy result or so).

The final attempt at finding the hoped for pattern of steady growth makes use of regression analysis rather than correlation coefficients. Here, instead of using merely the first and last figures for earnings in a period, for each firm a regression line is fitted to the earnings figures over the whole period. This means that for the values of earnings during the period a straight line is fitted in such a way as to minimise the distance of the observations from the line. (In these terms the correlation analysis fits a straight line by directly connecting the first and last observations, ignoring those in between. In each case the slope of the line represents the average rate of growth).

What are the advantages of this method over the previous one? First, it does take direct account of all the years in the period, and does not just consider the first and last, and therefore gives a more typical picture of what happens during the whole period. This leads to the second advantage, which is that it is not so open to the growth rate being upset by random fluctuations of the end points, though these will still have some effect on the slope of the line, especially since points far away from the average do again have considerable effect on the slope. However, the situation is improved, and the lines should not be so liable to considerable swings as the result of a single year's earnings. This brings us to the third point, which is the vital one of bias. Since first and last years have less importance in affecting the average growth, then with the use of non-overlapping periods the bias should be virtually eliminated. However, a combination of random factors causing a fall to very low earnings at the end of the first period, might then easily carry on to lead to a very large increase in the following period; and these, being large variations, could still cause some bias in the average rates calculated. To avoid this problem a further method could be used. This would be to use both absolute and logarithmic figures in the analysis.

In other words, the lines could be fitted to both the actual earnings figures, and the logarithms of them. This would result in obtaining both the average absolute rate of growth over the period, and also the percentage compound rate, as was used in the correlation analysis. Arithmetical figures are better, in so far as they avoid the problem of dealing with extraordinary rates of growth at low absolute levels of earnings; and they may also fit in better with actual management behaviour. It is difficult to be certain whether management thinks in terms of absolute or proportionate changes in sales or costs, though presumably the answer must be each to some extent. It is by no means certain, at least, that it is incorrect theoretically to use these absolute figures. However, there is still a statistical problem with absolute figures. Thus, in the case of the correlation analysis, this method could not be used, since, in order to calculate the coefficients, the growth of one period compared to the next was used for all the firms in the industry. If the absolute growth figures were used for this, then some significant relation might be found, simply because companies with high earnings would tend to have high earnings growth in absolute terms which might remain high in the second period, even if in percentage terms they were low relative to the rest of the industry. Therefore, there would be some danger of getting a spurious correlation due merely to the differing levels of firms' earnings. Although this difficulty does not arise when working out regression coefficients, it rears its head again when one comes to compare the different coefficients.

Therefore, in fact, a halfbreed method of dealing with the data was used. Instead of doing the regressions directly, using absolute or logarithmic figures, the earnings (pre-tax earnings per £1 nominal) of each year for each firm were divided by the average for the period of the regression. In other words, for each of the first six years, each firm's earnings were divided by its average earnings for the six years; and similarly for the figures of the last five years. The resultant regression coefficient is a kind of growth ratio, but such that the growth is compared with the average over the period, rather than with a previous year.[1] The series resulting from this method still contain some strong element of the simple arithmetic figures, since from year to year the changes are compared to a common base, and, therefore, the implication about managers' behaviour is rather similar to the remarks made above on the use of simple arithmetic figures. As far as statistical problems go, the use of these figures would seem to have the advantages of both arithmetical and logarithmic figures. Thus, all years are taken into account since regression analysis is being used; random fluctuations have much less importance than in the case of annual growth figures, since all changes are expressed as some ratio of average results which will not be a very low figure, and so the bias remains much reduced; and, finally, comparison of regression coefficients between firms will not lead to the spurious relationship caused by the different size of firms, since differences in earnings are still expressed as percentage changes whatever the size of the absolute level of earnings. There are still some problems concerned with using this series of figures, such as the fact that it appears to discriminate against growth, since any growth increases the average level of earnings, and pulls down the percentage changes throughout the period. In fact that is only the same effect as ordinary annual percentage growth figures have, since, with them, in the same way, early fast growth makes later growth small in percentage terms. Our method merely redistributes growth over the period for which it is being measured.

The final statistical question involved in the use of this method is the one of the length of period involved. This method has little advantage over the previous one unless the period over which the

[1] In order to help in the understanding of what follows, a regression coefficient of 0.1 means an average increase of earnings of 10 per cent (per annum) of the average earnings for the period.

growth rates are calculated is long. Obviously, for two years the methods are equivalent to each other. Therefore, the periods chosen were the longest possible; with the period of eleven years (1951–1961) at our disposal, we found the growth rates, for each of the firms with complete records, for the first six (51–56) and the last five (57–61) years. Limiting ourselves to this longest period meant that it was only possible to try and find out if there was some long run constancy in growth pattern; however this is inevitable using this method, and in any case there are so many problems involved in using any shorter period that it seems unlikely that it is possible to find any relationship. If such a relationship does exist in the short run, then it must be insignificant compared with the fluctuations that take place.

Therefore, for each firm in each industry with complete earnings records for the eleven years, simple regressions were done for the first six and last five years, regressing the figures for earnings, as a proportion of the average for the firm in the period of six or five years, against time. The coefficients resulting from this analysis are of interest for two reasons. First, there is the question of their size and sign as between the first and second period. So did the fastest growing firms continue to grow faster in the second period? Secondly, there is the significance of the co-efficients. If a large number of them are significant this implies

TABLE 1.9

Correlation of the average growth for the first six and last five years as obtained by regression analysis for each industry

Industry	No. of Firms	Corre- lation Coeffi- cients	Signifi- cance	Rank Corre- lation Coeffi- cients	Signifi- cance
Miscellaneous	40	.26	10%	.39	2½%
Motors	38	.24	—	.05	—
Stores	24	.08	—	.25	—
Cotton Textiles ...	21	−.45	5%	−.40	10%
Electrical Engineering ...	32	−.25	—	.08	—
Breweries	15	.15	—	−.03	—
Woollen Textiles	24	−.09	—	.01	—
Building	33	.18	—	.26	—
Chemicals & Pharmaceuticals...	23	.13	—	.25	—
Paper and Printing	23	.15	—	.13	—
Food	30	.47	1%	.33	10%
Mechanical Engineering (A) ...	50	.21	—	.05	—
Mechanical Engineering (B) ...	35	−.07	—	−.02	—

that there is, in fact, a tendency for there to be some actual steady growth relationship over the short period of six or five years, since this explains a significant part of the variation of earnings over this period. But it should be noted that this would include industry and general economic growth as well as between firm growth. This point is considered later.

It might be thought reasonable to consider the significance before the size of the coefficients; but, since the question of significance is much more difficult to interpret, and of a rather theoretical nature, we shall first consider the relationship of the size and sign of the coefficients between firms in the various industries. Even if these growth coefficients are not significant, they are still a better measure of the true average rate of growth (i.e., ignoring random factors) than using the first and last years only. This latter measures the actual average rate, which may be far off the true rate, due to the reliance on only two years.

The simplest use for these regression coefficients is to compare the values for the first and second periods, for each firm in the industry, by computing the correlation coefficients for these two figures. For the reasons stated above, this is not open to the dangers of obtaining a spurious result due to the size difference, since we are using a series of figures that has been deflated by the average for the period. The results are shown in Table 1.9, where the coefficients and significance (if any) are given for each industry in the first two columns of results.

The level at which the results are significant has been shown only where it is 10 per cent or above. The number of firms for each industry is basically the number that have complete earnings records throughout the period.

Though the majority of the correlation coefficients in the table are positive (9 out of 13), very few of them of either sign are significant. In an attempt to improve this, Spearman rank correlations were also done. These take account only of the position in the ranking of growth inside an industry, and thus ignore the size of growth in absolute terms. It was hoped that this might reduce the overwhelming effect that a few observations of large size have on the correlation coefficient. However, as can be seen from the last two columns of table 1.9, though the rank correlation coefficients may be a little more positive than the ordinary correlation coefficients, they do not appear to be any more significant. Some industry groups exhibit more of a tendency for steady patterns of growth, such as food and miscellaneous, whereas cotton textiles appears to have some strong reversal of the expected pattern. In neither case is the reason for this apparent. Cotton textiles as a group did badly over the whole period, but this does not explain why firms doing well relative to the rest of the industry in the first few years should do badly for the last few, and vice versa. The only case which may be easy to explain is the miscellaneous group, where the continuing pattern may be more due to changes between the industries included in this group, thus to a between industry effect, than to a between firm effect.

There is, however, one strange result that becomes apparent from close consideration of these results. In several cases it is the effect of one or two companies that causes the insignificant or negative coefficients; a few firms appear to bias the results considerably. Thus, in stores, the second ranked becomes last in the next period, and the last to begin with becomes third for the second period. Removal of these two raises the rank correlation coefficient to .63, significant at the half per cent level. In cotton textiles, the first ranked in the first period is last in the next. The removal of this one firm would considerably decrease the negative coefficient. In electrical engineering, again the first becomes last, and moreover the last two in the first period becomes the first two in the second period. Removal of these three would lead to a coefficient significant at the 5 per cent level. In breweries, the second becomes last, and the last becomes first. Removing these leads to a coefficient of .9. In woollen textiles, the last becomes second, and the last but one first, with a resultant coefficient significant at the $2\frac{1}{2}$ per cent. In building, the last becomes fourth and the second last, with a resultant coefficient significant at half per cent. Though these are the most impressive changes caused by a few firms, there is the same tendency in the other industries for there to be some firms which switch from a very high rank to a very low one, and vice versa. In all cases this has a large effect on the sign and significance of the rank correlation coefficients. Thus we seem to have a situation where there are a very few firms behaving violently in opposite ways over time, whereas the others behave more consistently.

One further piece of evidence that confirms the suggestion that perhaps some firms are different from others in some non-random way can be seen by considering growth rates as follows. A number of distributions, both for individual groups and for the whole sample, of the logs of the deviations of the growth rates, as used in the correlation analysis, relative to the mean growth rate, were plotted. They all showed a high degree of leptokurtosis—that is, the curves had much steeper and higher peaks, and longer tails, than normal curves of the same area. In other words, if the firms differed in their growth rates from purely random factors, then we should expect the distributions of these relative growth rates to be normal. However, in fact, there is some tendency for them to concentrate around the centre, leaving a few firms that have growth rates very far distant from the mean. These firms will have a very large influence on the correlation coefficients, and some at least will cause the negative bias described above.

However, this is not sufficient to prove that most firms are well behaved, and that the few others happen for some reason to upset the whole relationship. Certainly, some of the firms that have remarkable growth rates are also consistent from one period to the next, and help, rather than hinder, the positive correlation. Moreover, even if all the firms with high growth rates did behave in some perverse fashion, still we could not simply forget about them. It is very dangerous to remove some firms from a sample simply because they do not fit in with expected behaviour, and then to proceed to draw some conclusions about the rest. In this way one could prove anything! However, this particular case does appear to suggest such a distinction between firms, and, therefore, leads to the above tentative conclusion of the relatively reasonable behaviour of the majority. But, to be convincing, the erratic behaviour must be predicted by some other means than itself. In other words, for this result to be interesting or even useful, it must be possible to distinguish these wild firms from the others in some way separate from their wildness in the period in question. Without this demonstration it would be wiser to disregard this observed apparent result.

A confirmation of this curious behaviour was sent by Professor Edward Renshaw of the University of North Carolina as a comment on the original article. In this he reports on some U.S. companies' growth records. He considered the top sixty companies with the most spectacular rise in per share earnings between 1950–51 and 1955–56, and compared this with their rankings for the next 6

years. He found that 30 per cent of these 60 still lay in the top
20 per cent of the most popular 800 stocks, but that nearly a
quarter of them had fallen to the bottom 10 per cent of the 800.
In other words, he also found firms that behaved in strongly
opposite directions.

On the whole, these results may show a more positive relation
between growth and growth than the earlier ones, but they still
show a strange insignificance. Strange, because the concept of
insignificance implies that the values are the result of random
variations, and therefore should be distributed about zero
in a random fashion. However, of the insignificant results, 7 out of
10, and 9 out of 11 are positive, which is rather far off the even
distribution one would expect from the lack of significant coefficients. There are three possible reasons for this:—1. If each industry can be thought of as separate from the others, then it makes no
sense to compare one with the other. However, we must in fact
assume that they do behave in the same way, and that management
in one industry is not basically different from that in another.
2. It is, of course, possible that this distribution of positive and
negative could appear purely by chance with a random distribution
about zero, but this is not likely. 3. There may be some bias or
similar effect at work on the data or the calculations. If one
dismisses the first two reasons, then one has to accept this as the
cause. This perhaps reinforces the observations on wild firms
causing bias, but it is not clear that this is the real reason.

TABLE 1.10

Significance, size, and sign, of regression coefficients for industry groups

Industry	No. of Firms	First Period			Second Period		
		Significant Pos.	Neg.	Av. Coeff. for industry	Significant Pos.	Neg.	Av. Coeff. for industry
Miscellaneous ...	40	17	5	.032	15	4	.034
Motors	38	9	2	.022	10	4	.037
Stores	24	21	0	.110	12	5	−.035
Cotton Textiles ...	21	0	11	−.152	4	2	.062
Electrical Engineering ...	32	12	5	.023	10	5	−.004
Breweries	15	11	0	.058	9	0	.76
Woollen Textiles ...	24	5	4	−.021	6	2	.012
Building	33	13	4	.037	11	3	.029
Chem. & Pharmaceuticals	23	5	1	.033	9	2	.037
Paper and Printing ...	23	9	1	.012	10	3	.034
Food	30	19	2	.093	10	3	.021
Mechanical Engnrg. (A)	50	20	5	.039	11	14	−.039
Mechanical Engnrg. (B)	35	17	8	.019	10	12	−.068

This leads on to the even more difficult question of the significance of the 'significance' of the regression coefficients used in this analysis. Therefore, Table 1.10 shows for each industry, and for each period, the number of positive and negative statistically significant coefficients, and the average value of all coefficients.

The interpretation of Table 1.10 is rather difficult. First assume that the average of the regression coefficients were zero. With no relationship between earnings over time, we would expect to find 5 per cent of the regression coefficients significantly (at the 5 per cent level) different from zero. A positive relation between earnings over time (i.e. growth leading to growth, decline to decline) would mean a larger number of significant coefficients, both above and below zero. A negative relation of earnings over time (growth leading to decline, and vice versa) would not lead to significance, since the reversal of the direction of growth would make it unlikely that the fitted regression line would be far from the horizontal.

In the present case, we have about 50 per cent of the observations with significant coefficients, so it might seem that there is a positive relation between earnings over time. However, the foregoing paragraph was based on the assumption that the average of the regression coefficients was zero. In this case it is usually not zero, and therefore the picture is further complicated. What was said above would still hold true, but for significance measured away from the average value of the regression coefficient. Therefore, if this average is positive, it means that there will be positive regression coefficients that are significantly different from zero, but not from the average value: and similarly with negative coefficients. As can be seen from the table, almost all coefficients do follow the sign of the average (except stores in the second period). Does this mean that we cannot say anything about how many of these coefficients are really significant? We could calculate this, but this is not really necessary since we can deduce what we need by looking at the numbers of significant coefficients with the reverse sign to the average. This is already over 5 per cent, and the number must increase as we measure the deviation from the true average rather than from zero. Moreover, if we assume that the distribution of coefficients is more or less symmetrical about the average, then we can expect a similar number of significant coefficients on the other side of the average. This implies that there must be more than 10 per cent significant, and possibly 20 per cent or even more. There will certainly be a drop below the 50 per cent in the table, but there will be many more than the 5 per cent that would occur with no positive relation, and so such a relation seems proven.

There are two reservations on this result:—1. There is first the very difficult question of the earnings series used. If the figures that should have been used are the annual growth ones, then random behaviour of the firm would lead to a random walk path; i.e., its earnings growth would be independent of earlier years' growth, but would start from the earnings figure of the previous period. In this case, the use of absolute figures in regression analysis of the present type would lead to more than 5 per cent significant coefficients, even with a completely random walk pattern. Using mixed absolute and growth series, as was done in these regressions, will lead to this same result, and this could be the reason for our finding more than 5 per cent significant. However, one might reply that this is nonsense, since it is ridiculous to think of the change in earnings starting from the level of the previous year (itself partly a result of random fluctuations). Instead, it must start from some measure of earning capacity, and move from there. If this is true, some type of average (to measure this capacity) should be used, and the resultant series would move nearer to the one in our analysis, though, of course, it need not be exactly the same. In any case this would make the number of significant coefficients found greater than if the simple random walk hypothesis were accepted. It is perhaps weighting the case too much against the apparent short run growth relation that has been found, to compare it directly with a situation which demands that the manager must completely adjust to the previous year's earnings, in that further growth is measured from this. Any consistency in growth must surely be found over a longer period.

2. The second reservation to these results is much more simple. It is that, as stated earlier, any negative relationships will be hidden under the insignificant coefficients, and, therefore, even if there are a number of positive relations, there may be as many or more negative ones.

The conclusion of this section must be simply that there is the appearance of a positive relationship, but in the long run this is well camouflaged by some firms being violently contradictory, and in the short run by a great wealth of theoretical problems. There is certainly no clear proof of any positive relation; merely some very weak circumstantial evidence.

As a final use of the data, the following is a not too serious visual demonstration of its randomness, followed by a statistical sleight of hand using the identical results to show that in fact there is a very strong connection between the two periods' growth. This will prove either that it is impossible to see what is in front of your eyes, or else that statisticians should never be trusted. Consider Chart 1.12. In this, the ranks of the growth regressions inside each industry have been plotted on a scatter diagram, with the vertical scale representing the rank of growth in the first period, and the horizontal that in the second. The only alteration from the simple ranks, as used in obtaining the rank correlation coefficients, is that here they have been expressed as a proportion of the number of firms in the industry. This is necessary in order to make it possible to plot all the results on one diagram without the differing numbers of firms in the industries making the results very difficult to interpret. To give one specific example of what this diagram means, the point at .2 on the vertical scale and .6 on the horizontal represents a firm that is 2/10ths of the way down the ranking in the first period, and 6/10ths in the second. Therefore, if it is in an industry with 50 firms, its actual ranks would be 10th and 30th. Thus, the diagram shows at a glance the relation between growth in the two periods. A perfect positive relation with exactly the same ranking in each period would appear as a straight line of points up the 45 deg. line, whereas a completely random distribution would give an even scatter over the whole diagram. (There is one small reservation to this latter case, since there is no possibility of a point being on either zero axis, and therefore the scatter could not extend as far as this). A positive relationship plus a random element should show a concentration about a broad band along the 45 deg. line.

In fact, the diagram does seem to show a pretty even distribution over the whole area, though it might be possible to convince oneself of a slight tendency to concentration towards the centre band. It is also possible to see the small group of firms that caused so much trouble in the rank correlation analysis, by behaving violently in opposite ways in the two periods. They are those in the bottom right and in the top left of the diagram.

E

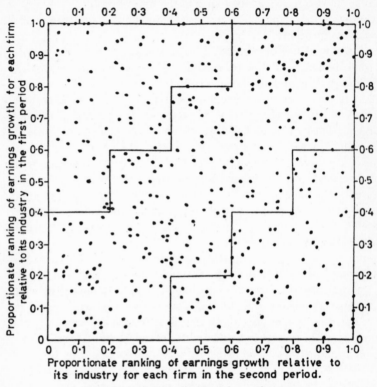

Chart 1.12. Scatter diagram of growth rates.

Whether it would have been justifiable to remove them from the calculations becomes even more doubtful on consideration of this chart, since, though they are grouped a little separately from the others, they do not really seem to belong to a different pattern. The only indication that this scatter is in fact not completely random is that, following any horizontal or vertical section across the chart, there does seem some slight tendency to concentrate in the area around the 45 deg. line. In order to test this apparently very weak tendency, the diagram was divided into 25 blocks, and the number of firms in each was counted. Firms located on the dividing lines were included in the block below and to the left, in order to compensate for the bias to the right and above due to the problem of the zero axis. In Table 1.11 the figures in the left of each block show the actual numbers of firms falling within the

TABLE 1.11

Numbers of firms falling in blocks of Chart 1.12

	L	M	N	O	P	Row Totals
A (1.0)	14 −1.6	10 −6.1	14 −1.7	17 .9	25 8.5	80
B (.8)	12 −3.1	15 −0.5	17 1.9	15 −0.5	18 2.2	77
C (.6)	13 −2.3	20 4.4	14 −1.3	16 0.3	15 −1.1	78
D (.4)	16 0.9	21 5.4	17 1.9	13 −2.5	10 −5.8	77
E (.2)	21 6.1	12 −3.3	14 −0.9	17 1.7	12 −3.6	76
Column Totals	76	78	76	78	80	388

Left hand figures in each block show the number of firms in the block, the right hand number being the deviation from the expected number. The column and row sub-totals of these deviations do not always add to zero, due to rounding.

Ideally, each row and column sub-total should be the same, since we are using percentage rankings on both axes. However, the fact that we have introduced arbitrary divisions in the diagram, added to the rounding bias, leads to some small variability in these sub-totals of up to 5 per cent. This can be allowed for in the calculations without any difficulty.

block. As can be seen from the column and row totals, there is still some tendency for the upward bias to the top right hand corner to remain.

If there were a completely random distribution of points over the diagram, then we can calculate how many we should expect on average in each block. The amount is not quite equal, due to the effect of the difference in row and column sub-totals, but in fact depends on the proportion of firms entering into the row and column that the block is situated in. Thus, the block at the top right can be expected to have more than any other, because its row and column have more in them than do any of the others; similarly, the bottom left should have the equal lowest number. From these calculated expected values the deviations of actual numbers from expected were calculated, and are shown at the right hand side of each block.

The figures were first tested with a Chi squared test to see whether these deviations were sufficiently large for us to be able to say that it is unlikely that they could have resulted from a random distribution over the diagram. This was only significant at a very low level, and therefore the distribution might easily have come about by chance. However, directly using this test on these figures of deviations takes no account of any pattern in them, and in fact, on inspection of Table 1.11, it can be seen that there is a tendency for the positive deviations to be centred around the 45 degree line, with the negative ones pushed into the top left and bottom right corners. In fact, blocks BO, CN, and EO, are the only direct exceptions to this pattern, that is three blocks out of twenty-five, and in each case the size of the deviation is small. Therefore, a second Chi squared test was done to see whether this pattern is in fact significant. The diagram was divided into two areas (shown as shaded and unshaded in Table 1.11), roughly showing those firms that do tend to keep a similar position in the ranking each period (that is the 45 degree blocks), and those that tend to reverse their position (the off-diagonal ones). It was again possible to calculate how many firms would be in each of these areas on average if there were a purely random distribution over the diagram, and therefore possible to test whether the deviation from this expected number was significant. In fact, it turned out to be significant at the 1 per cent and almost significant at the half per cent level. In other words, it is only one chance in just under two hundred that such a distinction between the two areas could have occurred with a random distribution. Since this result is based on the behaviour of all the firms in the sample, it appears to be a very strong result showing that there is a very significant tendency for firms to continue in a similar ranked position of growth over long periods.

It is perhaps not at all necessary to remind the reader of the warning concerning statistical sleight of hand that was given a few pages above. This apparently significant result comes from a scatter diagram that appears on casual inspection to show a very random distribution of firms, which certainly does not seem to fit in with this finding of a strong tendency for firms to remain as they are in ranking. First, some exception can be taken to the arbitrary way that the two divisions have been made, and the treatment of firms actually situated on dividing lines. But, even after this, there is still too strong a pattern for it to be dismissed out of hand. In fact the result must be accepted, but its implication must be understood, since in reality it is a very weak hypothesis that is being tested. It does *not* say that for any one firm there is only a one in two hundred chance that it will not continue to grow in the same position relative to the industry; nor does it even say that it will continue to have a rank very broadly similar in the two periods; nor even that there are these same odds on its behaviour being more likely to be consistent than inconsistent.[1] (In fact the odds do favour this, but only at about 5 to 4). All that the result really shows is that if all of the firms are taken and divided into consistent and inconsistent groups, then the consistent one is likely to be larger than an even distribution would suggest, at odds of 200 to 1. Therefore, if the reader invests in all the firms in this sample on the base of their growth ranks for a period of five or six years, then he will certainly be right in predicting the very broad ranking for the following five or six years more often than he is wrong. Not a very strong or useful result!

This is the only truly significant result that we have discovered in this investigation into growth consistency, and even this tells us very little of any importance. This weak tendency is certainly of such minuscule size compared with other factors affecting the

---

[1] The term 'very broad ranking' means dividing firms into groups of consistent and inconsistent ones. These latter mean the firms falling inside and outside the shaded area of Table 1.12.

growth of each firm that it can be all but ignored. The chart of
the ranks of growth must also throw doubts on the investigation of
correlations of regression coefficients, since the firms that have to
be removed in order to obtain many significant results are not
obviously different from the others. All the other results have
either been insignificant, or else so dependent on biases or assump-
tions of the importance of the biases, that it is hard to come to any
conclusion that there is some connection between past growth and
future growth, which is worth considering when either investing in
the market or pursuing some economic theory that uses the behaviour of firms. Though Marks and Spencers do exist, they either do not
belong to the group of firms we have considered, or else they are
just as likely to do badly next year as they are to continue to do
well. In fact, although we have cast some doubts on the usefulness
of the methods employed in the original article for discovering
connections between growth trends over different periods, nevertheless we have come to broadly the same conclusion—there is
virtually no tendency for growth trends over any time period to
repeat themselves.

(5). *The Influence of Size and Ploughback on Growth*

Though there seems to be very little sign of any non-random
pattern of growth, there still remains some possibility of there being
a pattern which we have been unable to detect. Therefore, it
is possible, but unlikely, that we can find some relationship between
size and growth. It is rather difficult to understand what such a
relationship would imply for the behaviour of a firm; if large firms
grow faster than small, then we should end up with one vast firm
that would have swallowed up all the others, since its absolute
growth must accelerate as it becomes larger. Alternatively, if the
larger firms grow slower than the smaller ones, then all firms should
tend towards the same ideal size—a result that does not seem to fit
in with observed facts. Admittedly, it is possible to think of a
situation where we could get an average relation between size and
growth, but where there are a few wild firms that might make it
possible to fit this relation in with the observed situation in
industry. However, this would be something of a statistically
freakish result.

Two possible size variables were available, the market value of
the equity, and the book value of assets. Since asset value is much

less sensitive to past growth, changing slowly and fluctuating less (so that the choice of time at which the size measure is taken is not critical), it was preferred to market value of the equity in spite of its well-known defects.

How in theory should growth be related to the amount ploughed back? Where e is the 'percentage earned for ordinary', g the rate of growth of earnings, d the dividend percentage, t the rate of tax, and p the rate of profit on money ploughed back, then the following formula holds provided that there is no change in the profitability of already existing assets:

$$g = p(1-t)\left(\frac{e-d}{e}\right).$$

$\frac{e-d}{e}$ was therefore chosen as the 'ploughback' variable.

The problem of lags presented itself, especially for this latter variable. If some firms have typically high dividend covers, the choice of lag would not matter. For one group (stores) a calculation was made to see how much of the sum of the squares of the deviations of the dividend cover[1] was accounted for by the deviations of particular firms about their own mean cover for the period 1951–59, and how much was accounted for by the deviations of these means from the mean of the set. We have:

(Deviations)² from own means = 16.15
(Deviations of own means)²   = 12.52

Rather a large part is thus accounted for by the year to year variability of each firm.

This means that, in fact, the proportion ploughed back by firms does vary considerably over time, so that it becomes less feasible to think of some firms as high ploughback firms, and some as low. At the same time, it becomes more possible that ploughback is a random variable, which could be related to earnings growth. The fact that the proportion ploughed back does vary over time, makes it of some importance to choose the correct lag in finding the relationship; however, lack of time prevented the use of any elaborate attempt at finding such an ideal lag.

[1] Where c stands for the dividend cover, $\frac{e-d}{e} = 1 - \frac{1}{c}$.

Trial regressions were done as follows:

$$X_1 = \frac{1959}{1958} \text{ (pre-tax earnings)}$$

$$X_2 = (\frac{e-d}{e}) \text{ in 1957}$$

$$X_3 = \text{asset size 1956 } (£1,000\text{'s})$$

There was no particular reason for choosing 1957. 1956 was chosen as the latest asset value which could not be affected by the ploughback. The regression equations were calculated for each 'industry', and for the entire sample.
Results were as follows:

1.   Ploughback Variable (X_2):
(a) Of 13 groups of large firms, the regression coefficient had the wrong sign in eight cases, but the coefficient was significant in none.[1]
(b) Of the 5 groups with the proper sign, only one was significant (electrical engineering)—probably a freak result.
(c) For the whole sample of large firms, the sign was both wrong and significant.
(d) For small firms, the sign was wrong but insignificant.

2.   Size Variable (X_3):
(a) Among the *13* groups (excluding the small firm group) the sign was positive in *7* cases and negative in 6—but significant in none. Indeed in 10/13 cases the standard error exceeded the value of the coefficient.
(b) For the whole sample of large firms, the coefficient was positive—but smaller than its standard error.
(c) Curiously enough, the coefficient was negative and significant (with a statistical probability of about 98 per cent), in the small 'group case. On the other hand it was very small.[2]

3.   Multiple Correlation Coefficient for the whole sample:
     Variance of $X_1 = .171597$
     Residual variance $= .171152$
     Variance explained $= .000445$
     Percentage of variance explained $= \frac{1}{4}$ per cent.

[1] That is, within two standard errors.
[2] The equation was $X_1 = 1.421 - .184X_2 - .000189X_3$.

Therefore neither size nor ploughback appear to have any affect on growth.

The fact that size has no apparent influence on growth is not very surprising, and confirms the work of P. E. Hart and S. J. Prais.[1] That ploughback has no apparent influence is rather more difficult to accept, and certainly more shocking. So further attempts were made to investigate this.

It seemed possible that, in some cases, the influence of ploughback on future growth might have been masked by a chance negative correlation of growth on growth, combined with the probability that high past growth would be associated, because of a lag in dividend adjustment, with high ploughback. For this reason, it was decided that a partial regression analysis of growth on ploughback and past growth should be undertaken.

It is worth noting also that partial regression analysis aims to eliminate the possible causative sequence, past growth → past ploughback→future growth, as well as the effect mentioned above. To this extent the partial regression may measure the influence of 'normal ploughback', that is ploughback which was not the result of a recent period of rapid growth. It seemed possible that 'normal ploughback' might be better related to future growth. Finally, the choice of a single year's growth, and a single year's ploughback, may have been unfortunate in the multiple correlation of growth on size and ploughback.

Accordingly, for two groups (mechanical engineering, dec. 31st; and mechanical engineering, others), growth for two years was related both to ploughback and to past growth.[2] The growth period chosen was $\frac{1959}{1957}$ (X_1), the ploughback taken was the mean for the three years 1955–57 (X_2), and the past growth period chosen was 1954–57 (X_3), since growth in these years might well influence the ploughback in 1955–57.

---

[1] *Journal of the Royal Statistical Society*, Series A, Vol- 119, part 2, 1956.

[2] For two groups (breweries and mechanical engineering, dec. 31st) the simple correlation coefficient between growth from 1952–59, and ploughback from 1951–58 was also calculated, to see whether over this long period any relationship existed. The relationship in each case was positive but weak. The correlation coefficient for breweries was 0.24, and for mechanical engineering, dec. 31st., was 0.18. In view of the long period of overlap these figures could easily be the result of dividend lag, and not arise at all from any real influence of ploughback on growth.

For mechanical engineering, dec. 31st, the correlation coefficients were:

$$r_{12} = -.05$$
$$r_{13} = -.08$$
$$r_{23} = +.24$$
$$r_{12 \cdot 3} = -.02$$

The partial regression coefficients were also, of course, negligible. For mechanical engineering, others, the correlation coefficients were:

$$r_{12} = .17$$
$$r_{13} = .16$$
$$r_{23} = .33$$
$$r_{12 \cdot 3} = .13$$

In this case $b_{12 \cdot 3}$ was positive and equal to .28 (expressing ploughback as a percentage)—i.e., other things being equal, an increase of 10 percentage points in the percentage of earnings ploughed back would raise the growth of earnings by 2.8 per cent. However, regarded as a random sample, this is not significant, for the standard error of $b_{12 \cdot 3}$ was .27. Our tentative conclusion from these two results is that there is no relation between ploughback and growth, even after making allowance for the independent influence of past growth on past ploughback and future growth. Obviously, however, this relation has not been exhaustively analysed.

(6). *Conclusions*

1. On whether there is any consistency in growth.

In the short run, it appears to be virtually impossible to find any growth consistency, because of the problem of bias upsetting all the investigations attempted. But this brings with it the implication that we cannot expect managements to readjust themselves, or their plant, in the short run, so that we can hardly expect there to be any continuation of growth from one year to the next. Their planning horizon is too long.

Over a longer period, we should expect there to be some such repetition of earlier behaviour, but this seems to be very hard to discover. In the several attempts made to find this relation many of the difficulties of bias have been overcome, but we still seem to be almost as far from discovering it as in the short run case. We have found, for certain, one very weak tendency for repetition of earlier growth; but this is so weak as to be negligible. All else seems to be non-existent, or else to rely on dubious hypotheses. Any unbiased reader of this chapter must come to the conclusion that there is no tendency for previous behaviour to be repeated in the future.

2. On whether the investment analyst is left with a job.

'In fact, broadly speaking, in assessing a company's future prospects the investment analyst needs to allow for the natural tendency for extreme earnings on capital employed to tend towards the average and in this situation, whilst the hypothesis of random growth becomes more acceptable, equally the investment analyst's approach based on critical examination of the past has some justification.' This sentence is part of an interesting article by M. G. Hall in *The Investment Analyst*, May, 1963, entitled 'Some thoughts on "Higgledy Piggledy Growth" '.

The article is, to some large extent, a defence of the position of the analyst, as well as a critique of the original article. With regard to the comments on statistical methods involved, the new additions in this chapter adequately answer most of the criticisms made on the analysis of growth. However, a point made concerning the heterogeneity of firms is of some validity. It is admitted that the grouping that we have used to divide firms into the 'industries' within which we have done our investigations by no means places firms only with their exact equals. Thus, there must be some element of 'between industry' differences in growth patterns entering inside the groups we have used. This was the central criticism in Mr. Hall's article, and therefore it is worth considering closely. If there is some cyclical pattern that differs for the various industries within the group, then this may lead to a negative correlation for some time periods. However, it will also lead to positive correlations with slightly differing lags or time periods. This is because the differing cycles will sometimes be moving in harmony, just as sometimes one is rising when the other is falling. Moreover, if one industry in the group has a trend relative to the others, then its firms will continue to do better, or worse, than the average, not because of their management, but because their industry group is moving in this way. Thus it seems rather more likely that the very real problem of heterogeneity will lead to a spurious positive correlation, than that it will decrease any such correlation as exists. Therefore, since we are not troubled by too large a positive correlation, it is not so important to be concerned with the problem of heterogeneity at this stage.

The comments on the correlation between ploughback and growth are accepted in part, though they do seem to fit in with the comments in the original article. The proportion of earnings growth explained by ploughback continues to be small, and there is the additional information given that there seems to be no relation between ploughback and earnings on capital. It is accepted that this portion of the original article does need more intensive analysis before it can become completely convincing.

To return to the title of this section, and the import of the quotation, what can the analyst do of value? The quotation is rather an underestimate of the strength of the implications of the original article. There is much more than a tendency for extreme earnings to tend towards the average; it would be more correct to say that there is no noticeable tendency for any earnings to move in any direction. What Mr. Hall means by 'a critical examination of the past' is not clear: but it should not be concerned with past growth of earnings, unless it also uses some extra factors related to something other than such growth. It is possible that the analyst can predict in the short run the relative movements of differing industries,[1] and so give some advice on the groups of shares to buy, but the evidence so far discovered seems to imply that there is little else that they can do in terms of predicting earnings—though one should admit that their main concern will be with prices.

3. On the economic interpretation of the results.

The failure to find either short or long run consistency of earnings growth is, perhaps, not quite so surprising from an economist's point of view. In the short run, it seems quite reasonable to suppose that fluctuations beyond the control of management should swamp any tendency to consistency that there might otherwise be. It is true that simple economic theory ignores the element of luck in determining profits, but then such theory is hardly supposed to be realistic.

Economic theory also usually abstracts from differences in the quality of management. If all management were equal, theory

---

[1] We have not tested whether there is any significant difference in the movements of industries. But Tables 1.3 and 1.4 suggest that there may be, although this would contradict the conclusions of Professor Barna (op. cit.)

suggests that the return on capital should tend towards equality in the long-run if competition is unrestrained. Such equality would never be realized, because there would always be some flow of completely unpredictable events. If we superimpose the notion of continuing good and bad management on top of this, then we would expect that there would be a long-run tendency for a higher return on capital to be achieved by good management. Since completely unpredictable events would strike good and bad managements alike, at any one time there should be a correlation between good management and a high return, although it would be far from a perfect correlation because of the disturbance caused by what was unpredictable.

A possible objection to the above might be that if the reason for a high rate of return was exceptional managerial ability, then the exceptional management would be in a position to secure for itself the extra earnings which it caused. Although the return on capital would be higher, this would be taken out in the fees of management, and would not show up in profits or, therefore, in earnings per share. However, in practice, it seems very unlikely that a superior manager, given somewhat conventional salaries, can secure the whole of the 'economic rent' attributable to his ability. Moreover, some of our firms are ones where the directors are large shareholders, so that there is little incentive to separate out the return to management from profits (indeed, there may be a tax advantage in not doing so). In practice then, it seems that good management should show up in a higher return on capital.

The presence of monopolistic elements in the economy would in theory have the same effect as superior management. There should therefore also be some correlation between monopoly power and the return to capital.

So far the argument has been static. If a firm has had its management, good or bad, for a very long time, then there is no change to be expected therefrom in earnings per share except in so far as more capital is invested per share. But, since an average firm ploughs back somewhere around half its net profits, there is in fact a continuous increase in capital per share (after adjustment, of course, for rights and scrip issues). We saw (p. 18, Chapter I) that, if there is no change in the profitability of old assets, then the growth rate of earnings per share is $p(1-t)(1-\frac{1}{c})$ where p, t, and c, stand respectively for the rate of gross profit on new capital, the tax rate, and the dividend cover. Since there seems to be no good reason to suppose any correlation between good management and either the tax rate or the dividend cover, it follows that consistent good management should show up in a consistent above average growth rate.

The same is partly true for monopoly power. A monopoly can in theory retain an above average return on capital provided that it does not try to grow faster than the market for its product. If this is growing only slowly, the monopoly must diversify or plough back rather little. Either way, the influence of its monopoly position on earnings growth is reduced. Moreover, it is probably rather rare to find a firm which has significant monopoly power over the whole range of its output. For this reason also, one would not expect monopolistic elements to have so strong an influence as good management in causing consistently high growth for some firms. We shall therefore concentrate on the lack of evidence of good management as being the more surprising.

We revert therefore to the questions we asked on p. 2, Chapter I. We now have, as we there presaged, shown that earnings growth occurs in an almost purely random manner. Further, we have just shown that if good managers secure a higher rate of return on capital than bad managers over a run of years, then earnings growth could not be random. Can we avoid the startling conclusion that there is no such thing as good and bad management, and that those firms which are thought to be well managed are in fact only luckily managed?

It is not very easy to avoid these conclusions, although a number of not altogether plausible let-outs suggest themselves.

First, it might be suggested that monopoly power and good management counteract each other. Monopolies do not earn high yields on capital because they are usually badly managed. The best managements do not earn high yields on capital because they are mostly to be found in the more competitive situations. Remember that performance has been judged relative to the industry, albeit not usually a very homogeneous industry. Now it is certainly true that within a conventionally defined industry, some firms, notably the biggest, may have more monopoly power than others. But that they should tend strongly to have such inferior management as to offset any such advantage does not seem too plausible, especially as they can probably pay better salaries. On the other hand it is the only explanation which kills both birds with one stone, and common observation does not really suggest that the most monopolistic public companies have been conspicuously good investments.

A second possibility, adumbrated on p. 2, Ch. I, is that the quality of the management changes rather rapidly from good to bad and back again. This could occur if the good managers skip rapidly from firm to firm. To some extent this happens. A change of management, or the calling in of company doctors, certainly sometimes produces a fairly short-lived but rapid rise in earnings, which cannot be expected to last since it is based on a sharp improvement in the profitability of existing assets. A picture in which the long-term background management is everywhere much of a muchness, but where the profitability of assets is from time to time and place to place jacked up by consultants or a new managing director, who does not stay for long, would not be inconsistent with our results. It is the longer-term above average earnings growth, which should result from a continuing management which succeeded in keeping the profitability of assets above average in the long-run, that we have failed to detect. We have seen that even competition should not prevent this happening.

A third possibility which might be suggested is that managements do not try to maximize earnings per share. It is, of course, often true that this is by no means their sole objective, and it may even be a minor consideration. This would mean that a successful management, and good in that sense, was not the same as good management from the shareholder's point of view. But we must be careful as to how far this could be any explanation of a random growth in earnings. We saw that non-random earnings would result if good successful management meant a higher than average return on capital. Suppose that the objective of management, whether in a monopolistic or competitive position, was merely to produce an average return on capital, and that they measured their success by other criteria—e.g. by increasing their sales, or their exports, or paying above average wages or benefits to employees?[1] But this theory of management would still not

[1] That managers seek maximum sales consistent with a normal return is a theory advanced by Prof. W. J. Baumol in *Business Behaviour, Value and Growth*. The Macmillan Company, New York, 1959.

tend to result in a random growth of earnings, for the successful managers would, over the longer periods considered, consistently get near to the desired return on capital. More generally, it seems impossible to think of any objective of management which could lead to random results.

Lastly, it must be admitted that we should not overstress the randomness of our results. On pages 44–46 Ch. I it was suggested that if a few firms with particularly erratic results between the two six-year and five-year periods were left out, then the remainder did behave in a moderately consistent manner, enough to produce significant correlations between the regression coefficients of the two periods. Of course, it is dangerous to leave out firms which are inconvenient for the theory under examination (that consistently good and bad management exists). But if special reasons, consistent with the theory, were often found to explain the erratic behaviour, then one would be on more solid ground. The obvious thing to look for would be a change of management in these firms, or a change in their competitive position. This has not been done.

To conclude, we do not claim to have shown that good and bad managers do not exist (nor that monopoly power does not exist). But we do seem to have shown that managements do not remain above or below average for very long—or, if they do, that such above and below average management can have so feeble an effect on earnings growth that we cannot detect it—and similarly for the monopoly power of firms. Certainly, investors are wrong to think that a few years' above average rise of earnings is evidence at all that good management, which will result in a continued rise, must be present. To the onlooker at least, the management's position seems to approximate to that of the general in *War and Peace*, himself mainly an observer watching the forces beyond his control deciding the outcome of the enterprise that he has initiated.

Chapter II

SPECULATORS OR INVESTORS?

(1) *Posing the Problem*

We saw in Chapter I that there appears to be little or no consistency in the growth of earnings amongst the larger firms in the country. However, this does not necessarily, of itself, imply that a person investing on the stock market can have no inkling of the future growth of his companies' earnings and dividends. There is still the possibility that he invests on the basis of facts, or feelings, which do not themselves depend on the previous years' growth of the company: and that these factors do in fact predict what will happen to the company in the years ahead. They will, of course, also have to follow some random path, in order to predict the random growth of earnings, but this is not an impossibility. Unless this is the case, he can be only a speculator, in the sense that whatever his intentions, all he is able to do is to predict, or rather to attempt to predict, the future changes in the price of his shares independently of the future changes in earnings. The question of whether he is able to foretell future prices will be dealt with in Chapter III; the first topic here is whether investors are able to predict the future financial state of the companies in which they put their money.

It may seem optimistic to talk in terms of predicting the future of a company; certainly there can be few people who would claim to be able to do this with any high degree of accuracy, but stated in a weaker form the proposition sounds much more feasible. Thus, many people would be happy to say that Butlins' or Marks and Spencer's earnings per share will grow faster than the average over the next year or so.[1] If this expectation is based on the past record of the companies in question, then Chapter I should have sown a few seeds of doubt. But perhaps it is actually dependent on some broader reading of the financial state of the companies, or on some trust in the sagacity of the directors,[2] or on a favourable

---

[1] This sentence was first written in the spring of 1964. Now (Dec. 1964) one would probably select another pair as examples of investors' confidence, which all goes to show!

[2] Lord Marks died after this was written.

F

view of the industry. If this is so, the reader may still believe that
he can say with some assurance that company 'A' will do better
than 'B' over the next year or two.

For the overall health of the economy, it would certainly
be desirable for money to flow more easily to those firms
that can best use finance for rapid expansion. Therefore, one
would like to see different yields on new issues being reflected in
their growth rates over the future years. This seems unlikely to be
the case unless there is the same relation of yields to future growth
for existing shares. If this is not so, then it would appear to
demonstrate that the market is of little value to the economy in
terms of redistributing money to the firms that are most in need of
it; though it may still be of value in controlling the flow of funds
over time, or in permitting the investor to put his money into a
company or industry without committing himself to it indefinitely.
This adds to his peace of mind and liquidity. Also the market does
give the gambler's instinct, present in most people, a cheap and
satisfactory outlet.

Before leaving the market merely with the problem of chasing
its own tail, as it were, let us examine the question of whether in
fact the public's expectation of the future of a firm bears any significant resemblance to what actually does happen to it. There are two
immediate problems to be faced before starting. The first is the
simple question of whether an investor's optimism or pessimism
about a firm is at all affected by his expectation of the financial
future of the firm; he may be solely interested in his expectation of
future price changes. To the extent that this is the case, and his
expectation is independent of future financial changes, then the
question asked in this section is already answered. But if his
expectation of a future rise in price depends, even subconsciously,
on the future growth of earnings per share of the company, then,
if he is correct in his expectations, his optimism should be reflected
in the actual future financial state of the company. Therefore,
though it is unlikely that a person's attitude to a particular firm
depends only on his expectations of its profits and dividends in the
future, it is extremely likely that a considerable part of this
attitude must be related directly, or indirectly, to these expectations. The second section of this chapter deals with the question of
whether we can easily discover where an investor gets his expectations from.

The second problem is more one of application, and is simply the question of how we can tell what the attitude of the investing public is towards any particular share. It is immediately apparent that merely considering the market prices of shares is not any help, since factors like differing dividends and nominal values will make nonsense of this approach. (Despite this, there is believed to be an irrational dislike of 'heavy' shares.) It is more reasonable to consider the yields on shares as some measure of the market's expectation of the future of the companies in question, since differing yields should reflect the degree to which people are optimistic or pessimistic about the particular shares. However, at any one time, there will be more information about some companies than others. Thus, a firm that is six months away from an annual report (ignoring the possibility of interim statements) has more unknown factors than one which published its report in the previous week, and therefore, there is more of a speculative element in its yield than in that of the second firm. To avoid this speculative element, it is better to compare the yields that exist in the period following the publication of the financial statement for each firm. To avoid the further problem of differing dates of publication, implying that yields at differing times must be compared, when there may have been a change in average yields meanwhile, it is best to compare the relative yields of the shares. Therefore, the final comparison is between the yields of the shares soon after the publication of the annual statement, as a proportion of the average market yield at the same time.

If investors take a long run view of the prospects of a company, they will not completely alter their expectations on the publication of the new dividend figures, and therefore the price will not move proportionately with the dividend. The result of this will be that the yield must change. In other words, the yield index, since it uses only the current year's dividend, may give an incorrect indication of the expectations of the investor who considers a longer period than this. Specifically, this will lead to greater fluctuations in the yield index than would be the case if actual expectations were known. However, this is true only if people do evaluate the share over a long period; and we can take account of it to some extent by taking the average of several years' yield indices. This will not be the same as using an index employing an average of several years' dividends in calculating each yield index, but it is hoped that the two will not be too different. In any case, this problem should only reduce the efficiency of prediction, not bias the direction.

A further problem of adjustment to dividend figures occurs within the period of one year, rather than over several years as considered in the previous paragraph. The problem is to know when the market has adjusted to the new dividend news in so far as it is going to adjust. Does the report of a dividend figure cause instantaneous adjustment to the new 'correct' price, or is there a long lag of adjustment, or even an overcorrection for the change that is then readjusted as a few more weeks pass? How soon after the publication of the accounts can we consider the appropriate time for observing the yield figure? Mr. M. F. G. Scott has done some work on this question.[1] He related earnings yields to past earnings growth, and other factors—the results of which we will discuss later. However, he also regressed these variables on earnings yield at different dates relative to the date of the publication of the accounts. The following are the multiple correlation coefficients that he obtained for various times.

Date	Value of Multiple Correlation Coefficient
Day before publication of final dividend	0.716
Day after publication of final dividend	0.757
One week after publication of final dividend	0.748
Three months after publication of final dividend	0.691
Eleven months after publication of final dividend	0.556

The fact that the best fit was obtained for the earnings yield figures of one day after the publication of the final dividend, suggests that the market does adjust quickly to the announcement, so that using the figures for the period immediately following publication does seem to be the best, though there may still remain some problem due to the question of lags in adjustment to the correct market price. It is also interesting to note that there can be little variation in market price resulting from the announcement of the dividend, since there is only a small improvement in prediction of earnings yield between the day before the announcement and the following day. This implies either that investors are able accurately to predict what the dividend is going to be, or else that they do not react very much to the announcement.

[1] See foreword.

However, this will be considered at greater length in the second half of this chapter, when we will look at the factors that affect the earnings yield. Though we cannot say that this problem of knowing which is the best time to observe the yield index is of small importance, it is hoped that we have minimized it, and that any resultant bias will be small.

Moodies Security Indices and Charts Service contains a 'yield ratio' of the type discussed above. This is the proportion which the yield on an individual share bears to the average yield of their general equity index of sixty representative industrials. These ratios are based on the yields at the time of the publication of the annual accounts, and so should, for the reasons mentioned above, have similar degrees of speculative considerations affecting their yields. The deflation of the yields for each firm by the overall average yield does itself introduce a problem. This is that if a particular industry, say stores, tends to have a trend or cyclical variation in its average yield which is different from the trend or cyclical variation in the overall average of yields, then deflating firms in the stores group by the overall average will lead to an incorrect estimate of the market's evaluation of the firms *vis à vis* their market average, because they are being deflated by a different average than their own. Similarly, when there is some trend over time making one group more popular than the average, then deflating by the overall average will again give a wrong impression of the attitude of the market to the firm relative to its group. However, this would not matter if all the firms in the industry were deflated by the same wrong average, since we are concerned only with the relative appreciation of each firm. In other words, each firm would be incorrectly evaluated compared with the true average of the industry, but would be correctly evaluated relative to the other firms which have also been deflated by the same incorrect average. However, since in fact the firms have their yields deflated by the overall average at different times of year, this will lead to an incorrect estimate of one firm relative to the others in the industry. Thus, each firm's yield index will contain both between industry and within industry elements. Since the between industry part will vary over the year, this means that a comparison of the earnings yields of firms in an industry, which publish their dividends at different dates, will include an element caused by the relative movements of the industry and overall averages, as well as the between firm element that we hoped to observe. The strength of this element will depend on the relative movements of the public appreciation of differing industries. This problem would disappear if the yields were instead deflated by their own industry averages. However, there would be problems in deflating by these, particularly in industries with a small number of firms, and in fact the difficulties caused by using the overall average cannot be large, and will lead only to a somewhat larger inaccuracy and not to a bias. Therefore, the use of Moodies Yield Index seems justified, especially since it is hardly likely that we are expecting very accurate predictions by the investor, though we shall have to hope that the between industry factor is small, or does not vary much over the year.

The simple question to be answered is whether this index of relative yields is of any value in telling us whether the company will do better or worse than the average in the future; in other words, whether the investing public in its market reaction to a company's annual statement is able to see what the company actually is going to do in the next few years. There is no question for the moment of foretelling how the share price is going to vary, just that of having some estimate of how earnings and dividends will change for one firm compared with the industry average over some period of time.

(2) *A Visual Approach*

Before analysing the overall statistics of the relation between the yield index and future changes in earnings and dividends for the whole selection of firms, let us first examine some firms from one industry graphically, and see whether there is any strong obvious visual relationship. In Chart 2.1, there are plotted, for six stores, the paths over time of the yield indices, and series representing the growth of earnings and dividends. Before explaining what these series are it must be emphasised that these charts cannot be taken as typical of the stores industry, or of the whole sample of firms. Each of the six was chosen for particular reasons, either to illustrate some type of relationship, or because they are favourites with the market. Therefore, it will not be possible directly to apply any patterns seen here to the market as a whole, without first considering some statistical tests based on the whole group of firms. However, it is possible that in observing the actual

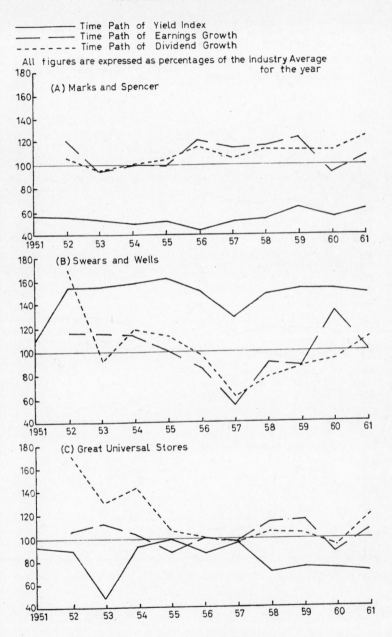

Chart 2.1. Market valuation and financial growth of various stores.

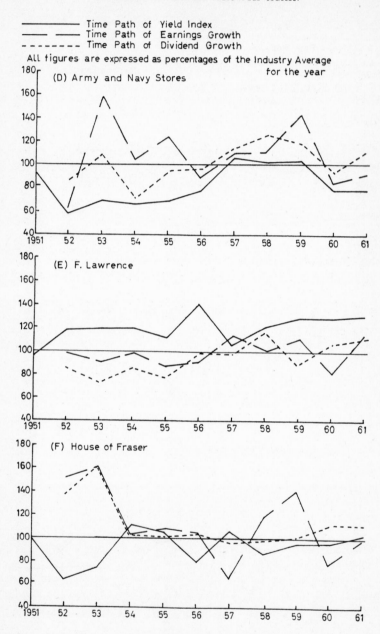

——————— Time Path of Yield Index
——— ——— Time Path of Earnings Growth
- - - - - - - Time Path of Dividend Growth

All figures are expressed as percentages of the Industry Average for the year

(D) Army and Navy Stores

(E) F. Lawrence

(F) House of Fraser

Chart 2.1 (continued). Market valuation and financial growth of various stores.

variations of a few firms, factors will appear that would be lost by a direct attempt to link statistically the yield index with earnings and dividend growth.

The yield index expresses investors' expectations for a particular company relative to the other firms included in the index. For the moment we are concerned with the question of whether investors can predict the behaviour of firms over time within one industry, rather than the various fluctuations between industries, which we will consider later. Therefore, we require the yield index to show us investors' expectations of the firm, relative to the rest of the industry. Consequently we must remove the between industry evaluation element in the yield index. This is done by expressing the yield index every year for each of the six stores as a percentage of the average yield index for that year of the twenty-six firms included in the group of stores. Similarly, the other two series express the growth in earnings and dividends as a percentage of the average growth in the industry for the year in question. Therefore, a yield index value of one hundred means that the yield on the firm's shares that year was the same as that for the group of all stores, whereas a value of fifty implies a yield half that of the average. So, the lower the yield index time path, the more the public are expecting the firm to do well in the future. On the other hand, a low value for the earnings and dividend growth paths means that the firm is in fact doing worse than the average. (The yield index series starts one year earlier than the others because they require the previous years' figures to form growth ratios.)

The first noticeable feature of these six charts is that there seems to be some definite market attitude to these companies, which may or may not be justified. Thus the yield index path for Marks and Spencer (A) is consistently very low, while that for Swears and Wells (B), and F. Lawrence (E), are both high for virtually the whole of the period. In fact, apart from House of Fraser (F), there is no doubting the market's attitude to these companies, which perhaps suggests a certain amount of consistency, or long run appreciation, by the investor, though it should again be emphasised that these shares were not chosen as being representative of the whole market, but rather to illustrate various forms. Thus, Marks and Spencer was the growth stock in terms of market expectation, and Swears and Wells the unpopular share.

To what extent are these expectations fulfilled? In the case of
the popular companies, A, C, and D, the record of the financial
achievement is not as consistent as the market evaluation. Even
the highly prized Marks and Spencer has an earnings record at, or
below, average for the years '53, '54, '55 and '60, though admittedly
not far below. However, it is the most consistently good of the six
companies represented here, which may be some justification for
such a low value of the yield index. Any definite conclusion as to
the overall relation of performance and valuation is impossible to
state from these graphs, though it is possible to convince oneself
that the popular firms do better than the unpopular on the whole.

Certainly, it is noticeable that the time paths of the yield index
and earnings growth usually do not cross each other, which might
be a sign of valuation predicting overall behaviour. But closer
inspection of the variations of earnings around the average line
makes this phenomenon appear to be a result rather of the consistent market evaluation of these companies, which keeps their
yield index time paths safely out of the way on one side or other
of the average line.

It is the year to year fluctuations that hinder any attempt to
see some clear-cut relationship, and so it is worth asking whether
the market is able to predict these short term variations. If it did,
then the pattern that would be seen would be the yield index time
path mirroring that of the earnings growth, but with this mirror
image preceding the pattern in the earnings growth. However,
though one can perhaps see a mirror image in C and F, it is
equally easy to see that in B and D the paths follow the same
pattern, which would imply that as a company becomes more
popular, so its results become worse! As to the question of the
variations in the yield index preceding those in the earnings
growth, this is impossible to observe in these graphs.

In fact, the only clear relationship to be seen is that earnings
and dividends tend to stick together, but with dividends tending
to be more stable. This, of course, fits in with our expectation of
firms' behaviour. On the topic of dividend growth there is one
rather interesting problem. This is the question of whether it is
possible to connect the value of the yield index directly to the
expected rate of growth of dividends relative to other firms. Thus
the yield on Marks and Spencer stays at a value around sixty
per cent of the average. Why? In the short run, because investors

expect its price to rise more than the average; but, in the long run, ignoring the remote possibility of the firm being taken over, it must be because its dividends are expected to rise faster than the average. Even if the price is high now because it is expected to be higher later, this price rise can hardly be expected to continue for any long period of time, unless it is also expected that dividends will be raised again. In other words, yields are relatively low now since dividends are expected to rise faster in the future. So, the shareholder is allowing his expectation of higher future dividends to compensate him for his small receipts now. We can see from the yield index figures just how much the investor is giving up in the present. Therefore, allowing for some risk compensation, we can find out how much he expects to gain in the future from the relatively rapid expected growth of dividends. Unfortunately, it is difficult to move from this stage to that of actually saying how much he is expecting the dividends to rise, since the investor is, if rational, equating his loss of dividends now with the 'present value' of the expected higher dividends in the future, and this 'present value' depends on the amount he values receipts in the future—his own rate of 'time preference'. This rate is difficult to estimate.

However, reversing the procedure, it is possible to work from your own time preference rate and expectation of the rise in dividends, and arrive at a figure of what you think the yield index of a certain share should be. From this it is easy to see whether the market valuation is too high or too low in your opinion. This is merely a slightly more scientific approach to what most investors, as opposed to speculators, do: that is, it concentrates more on the level of the price than on expected changes from the present level. Of course, this procedure makes sense only if there is little variation in the trend of dividend movement. Since dividends cannot grow for long without a similar movement in earnings,[1] it would appear that the findings of Chapter I preclude this rational approach to investment and the determination of yields, unless investors successfully base their expectations on something more than past experience.

The question of whether it is in fact possible to base these

---

[1] Starting from the exceptionally high dividend cover of the early post-war period, and given some tax reductions, some companies have in fact increased their dividends for a decade with little or no earnings growth. But they were exceptional, and so was the period in this respect.

expectations on anything else, has so far been examined by merely looking at the above charts. Let us now examine from a more statistical viewpoint the question of whether there is any significant relationship between the yield index and future growth of earnings or dividends.

(3) *The Statistical Analysis*

The first problem is that of time period: over what length of time is the investor expressing his expectations when he thinks that a certain yield is the correct one for a particular firm? Is he predicting the figures for the following year, or is he trying to forecast over a period of five or six years?

The second problem is rather serious, and difficult to deal with. This is because there is no one-way reaction between earnings and the yield index. Presumably, past growth in earnings does affect the yield index, while at the same time the latter may be able to predict their future growth. Because of this we have to be very careful when we regress the two variables together, so that what we get is the relation we want, rather than the inverse of the other. Thus, if we regress $E(t+1)/E(t)$ (earnings in the year $t+1$ divided by earnings in the year t) on $Y(t)$ (the yield index in the year t), we would hope that there would be a negative relationship between the two, implying that a high yield successfully predicts a lower than average growth of earnings. However, we can also expect there to be a negative relation between $E(t)/E(t-1)$ and $Y(t)$, since growth in earnings will probably lead to an optimistic evaluation of the share, and therefore a low yield.[1] This second relation implies a negative relation between $E(t)$ and $Y(t)$, i.e., given last year's results, an increase in earnings will tend to decrease the yield index. This implies a positive relation between $E(t+1)/E(t)$ and $Y(t)$, which will work against our desired negative one. To avoid this conflict, the minimum prediction period taken was two years. In other words, we aim to find out whether the yield index this year can predict the growth of earnings or dividends in the year following this one. In fact, from the results of Chapter I, it is very optimistic to expect to be able to predict earnings growth for one year, since we already know that it fluctuates a great deal.

---

[1] Of course, the questions asked on page 67–8 of this chapter will make this second relation less perfect, but, as shown in the latter half of this chapter, and by Mr. Scott (loc. cit.), it certainly exists.

In the succeeding statistical analysis the full period of eleven years was used, from 1951 to 1961, so the firms included are only those with complete records for earnings, dividends, and yield index, for the whole period. To begin with, a cross section analysis was done, i.e. it was investigated whether the market could decide between firms in each group as to which would give the better results. The figures used, as explained earlier, were the yield indices of the companies' shares, and the growth of earnings and dividends as a proportion of the growth in the same industry over the same period. Three periods were considered, short, medium, and long, and the first object was to find some relationship within each industry. In the short period, for the years 1953 to 1961, $E(t)/E(t-1)$ was regressed on $Y(t-2)$ for each industry, the earnings figures being adjusted for the average change in the industry as a whole. This resulted in nine regression coefficients for each industry. For the medium period, $E(t)/E(t-2)$ was regressed on $\frac{1}{2}[(Y(t-3)+Y(t-4)]$, i.e. the growth over the last two years was related to the average of the yield index for the previous two years, again avoiding overlap for the reasons stated above. This could be done for the years 1955 to 1961, a total of seven regression coefficients for each industry. Finally, in the long period, the growth for the last five years was regressed on the average of the

TABLE 2.1A

Regressions of Earnings Growth on Yield Index

Sign and significance of regression coefficients.

		Short run				Medium run				Long run			
				Sig.	Sig.			Sig.	Sig.			Sig.	Sig.
D.F.	Industry	Pos.	Neg.	Pos.	Neg.	Pos.	Neg.	Pos.	Neg.	Pos.	Neg.	Pos.	Neg.
35	Miscellaneous ...	2	7	1	2	2	5	0	0	0	1	0	0
34	Motors... ...	6	3	0	0	3	4	1	0	0	1	0	0
24	Stores	3	6	0	3	1	6	0	3	1	0	0	0
17	Cotton Textiles ...	5	4	0	2	5	2	0	1	1	0	0	0
26	Elec. Engrng. ...	8	1	2	0	6	1	0	0	1	0	0	0
10	Breweries ...	5	4	1	1	5	2	0	0	1	0	0	0
18	Wool Textiles ...	4	5	0	0	2	5	0	0	1	0	0	0
25	Building ...	3	6	1	1	3	4	1	0	1	0	0	0
21	Chemicals and Pharmaceuticals	4	5	0	0	1	6	0	1	0	1	0	0
19	Paper & Printing	2	7	1	0	1	6	0	1	1	0	0	0
28	Food	4	5	1	1	3	4	0	0	0	1	0	0
43	Mech. Eng. (A) ...	5	4	2	1	4	3	1	0	1	0	0	0
26	Mech. Eng. (B)	6	3	1	0	5	2	2	0	1	0	0	0
	TOTALS ...	57	60	10	11	41	50	5	6	9	4	0	0

yield valuation for the first six years in order to see whether the market could predict over a period of many years. This, of course, yielded only one regression coefficient for each industry. The whole series of regressions was repeated using figures for dividend changes instead of earnings changes. The results are shown in Tables 2.1A and 2.1B.

TABLE 2.1B

Regressions of Dividend Growth on Yield Index

Sign and significance of regression coefficients.

D.F.	Industry	Short run		Sig.	Sig.	Medium run		Sig.	Sig.	Long run		Sig.	Sig.
		Pos.	Neg.	Pos.	Neg.	Pos.	Neg.	Pos.	Neg.	Pos.	Neg.	Pos.	Neg.
35	Miscellaneous ...	4	5	0	3	2	5	0	0	0	1	0	0
34	Motors... ...	3	6	0	3	1	6	0	3	0	1	0	0
24	Stores	3	6	0	5	2	5	0	5	0	1	0	1
17	Cotton Textiles ...	3	6	0	1	2	5	0	0	1	0	0	0
26	Elec. Engrng. ...	3	6	0	1	5	2	0	1	1	0	0	0
10	Breweries ...	4	5	0	1	2	5	0	1	0	1	0	0
18	Wool Textiles ...	1	8	0	1	0	7	0	0	0	1	0	0
25	Building ...	1	8	0	0	2	5	0	0	0	1	0	0
21	Chemicals and Pharmaceuticals	2	7	0	2	1	6	0	1	0	1	0	0
19	Paper & Printing	2	7	0	3	0	7	0	2	0	1	0	1
28	Food	2	7	0	1	1	6	0	2	0	1	0	0
43	Mech. Eng. (A) ...	2	7	1	2	2	5	0	2	0	1	0	1
26	Mech. Eng. (B)	2	7	0	0	3	4	0	0	1	0	0	0
	TOTALS ...	32	85	1	23	23	68	0	17	3	10	0	3

In these tables, the columns contain the following:

First, the number of 'degrees of freedom' in each industry, a figure which gives some idea of the usefulness of applying this statistical analysis. (In fact, apart from breweries there are an adequate number of degrees of freedom in all these industries, and even the case of breweries is not so bad as to be not worth considering); secondly, the name of the industry, and then for each of the three periods, figures for the number of positive and negative regression coefficients (the sign showing the direction of the influence of the yield index on the other variables), and figures showing how many of these coefficients are significant (i.e. having only a 5 per cent probability that the coefficients could be as large as they are by chance alone).

Consider Table 2.1A, the regressions of growth of earnings on the yield index figures. Here the market seems to be very inefficient at predicting the earnings growth of firms. The total figures show that for short, medium, and long run periods, if the market became optimistic about some share, the earnings of the company fell almost as frequently as they rose! The totals of the significant coefficients are also distributed evenly between the two signs. (There is a larger proportion of significant coefficients than one would expect from chance alone, 14 per cent instead of 5 per cent; but these are divided so evenly that it does not upset the apparent failure of our attempt to discover a negative relationship).

Amongst the industries, miscellaneous, and paper and printing, do best, each having 13 negative as against 4 positive coefficients. However, some variation between industries is to be expected due to random factors. Moreover, each of the three time periods is bad, though the longest seems to be worse than the other two. All in all, it seems that the market is no good at predicting earnings.

But what of dividends? Is the market any better here? Judging from Table 2.1 B it is very much more successful. In total, there are 163 negative and 58 positive coefficients, a difference that cannot be due to chance. Moreover there is only 1 positive and 43 negative significant coefficients. Amongst the different industries only electrical engineering has more positive than negative coefficients, whereas wool textiles has only one positive value. Again, considering the three time periods, there is little difference in terms of the distribution of signs and significance. So, the investor appears to be able to predict relative dividend growth, but not relative earnings growth. Unfortunately, this is rather against the normal expectation that earnings and dividends move along similar paths (as stated, for example, when discussing Chart 2.1). If both financial variables do move together, how is it possible for the same variable—the yield index—to predict one, but not the other?

Before considering this difficult problem, there is one other thing that should first be examined. The figures given in Table 2.1 answer the question of whether it is possible for the market to discern between firms inside one industry. However, the decision facing the investor includes choosing between firms from differing industries. To see whether this is any easier than from the same industry, all we need do now is to find out if the market can foretell the financial future for industries as aggregates. If they can neither predict the relative behaviour of firms inside an industry, nor of one industry relative to another, then they will not be able to predict the future of firms from different industries. Therefore, the same analysis, as outlined above, was done using the industry average growth figures, and the industry average yield index figures, and treating each industry over the whole economy in the same way as the firms within one industry. For this analysis, there were 13 values of the variables for each year. The results are shown in Table 2.2, in the same manner as before, except that the earnings and dividend results are now in one table.

TABLE 2.2

Inter-Industry Regressions of Earnings and Dividend Growth on Yield Index
Sign and significance of regression coefficients.

| | | Short run | | | | Medium run | | | | Long run | | | |
| | | | Sig. | Sig. | | | Sig. | Sig. | | | Sig. | Sig. | |
D.F.	Industry	Pos.	Neg.	Pos.	Neg.	Pos.	Neg.	Pos.	Neg.	Pos.	Neg.	Pos.	Neg.
11	Earnings growth	6	3	2	1	3	4	1	2	1	0	0	0
11	Dividend growth	3	6	1	2	2	5	1	2	0	1	0	0

The results are very similar to those for the within-industry regressions, with the coefficients of the earnings growth regression tending to be distributed fairly equally between positive and negative, while those for dividend growth are quite strongly biased in the negative direction, though there are too few degrees of freedom for this to be statistically significant. It does appear that the pattern of the market's ability to predict is similar when choosing between industries, as when it is picking firms inside one industry. Therefore, there is the same strange result which seems to imply that earnings and dividends are independent of each other. Is this possible?

Closer inspection of Table 2.1 shows that parts A and B are not so independent as first seems to be the case. Although the results in A are much more equally balanced between positive and negative than in the case of B, still the order of successful forecasting is similar in both parts. Thus, electrical engineering is the industry that the investor has least success with, in trying to forecast both earnings and dividends: in the first case, 15 positive coefficients against 2 negative; and in the second, 9 positive against 8 negative. (In fact, this is the only industry in B where the market predicts wrongly more often than rightly). Measuring the relative efficiency of prediction between the two tables by merely correlating for each industry the number of successes in the two parts of the table, produces a correlation coefficient of .67 which is significant at the 2 per cent level. In other words, although the investor can predict dividend growth much better than earnings growth, which he seems to be no good at, he still seems to have the same order of successes with the different industries in each attempt at prediction.

It is certain that earnings fluctuate much more than dividends; although earnings may follow something like a random walk path as suggested in Chapter I, dividends will follow them in a much smoother path as a result of the policies of boards of directors. Especially in the short run the board is likely to follow its own dividend forecast somewhat independently of the earnings results, and over a longer period there is still likely to be a discernable, and therefore predictable, trend in dividend growth. Indeed, it is possible that the dividend policy of a company will be affected by the confidence of the market in it. So it is not too surprising that the market can predict dividend growth with some success; for it is to some extent predicting the policy of the directors rather than the financial condition of the company. Nor is it surprising that it is unable to predict the earnings growth since this follows too random a pattern for the market to be able to tell what will happen to it. In the very long run, dividend change must follow earnings, and both should be equally predictable or unpredictable, but this period seems to be longer than the five year prediction period of the long run regressions in these calculations; possibly longer than one would intuitively expect. Finally, we must ask whether these comments are consistent with the similarity of the patterns of success in the two groups of regressions?

This is rather a difficult question. For example, if the market is no good at predicting earnings growth, what does it mean to talk about the order of successful prediction between industries? Or, to reverse the question, if there is a similar industry pattern in the success of prediction in both dividends and earnings, then does not this suggest that there must be some measure of success for earnings also? In other words, the distribution of efficiency of prediction between the various industries in the earnings regressions seems to be more than merely following a random pattern, which suggests that the prediction of earnings is not quite so random as at first seemed the case.

G

The most likely explanation for these two seemingly inconsistent results, is that there is some bias operating on the earnings predictions, but not on those for dividends. If this were the case, then it might be possible for people actually to be able to predict what was going to happen to earnings, but for the bias to work against this predictive ability, until the observed prediction was wrong as often as it was right. But, what could be the cause of such a bias? Theoretically, it could operate either in the market itself, or in the statistical analysis. However, the former possibility implies a quite ridiculous mode of behaviour on the part of the investor. He would have actually to reverse his expectation to some extent; not simply reduce it, which might be quite reasonable in terms of being safety minded. Moreover, even apart from this question of the implied stupidity of the investor, we would then be left with the problem of how he could be efficient about predicting dividends. Therefore, there would seem to be no possibility of the bias appearing in the market. If it does exist, it must be in the statistical calculations.

One thing that might cause this was described above on page 76, but the time periods used have been chosen to try and eliminate this problem, and in any case, since both dividends and earnings are dealt with in the same way, the amount of bias would be the same for each, or rather, slightly larger for the dividend prediction, since the dividend figures are more directly connected to the yield index.

A second 'explanation' of the relative efficiency of the two predictions is simply to state the fact that the market is markedly less apt at predicting the future of earnings, but that it can still make some attempt at it, and be more successful in some industries than others. This is more of a description than an explanation, and still leaves us with the question of why there is the similarity in patterns of prediction between earnings and dividends. To answer this question, it is necessary to give some further thought to the relationship between these two. Since the same variable—the yield index—is being used to predict both of the future growth figures, and since we expect some connection between earnings and dividends, we should expect a similar pattern of prediction for the two of them. Indeed, we might suggest that the fact that the market has any success at all with earnings is due to its success with dividends and the link between them and earnings. This explanation would be more convincing if there were a strong correlation between these two variables, especially in the industries where the market was relatively efficient at earnings prediction. Unfortunately, however, the correlations between earnings and dividends do not follow (at least on the aggregate level), a pattern at all similar to that of the successes at predicting earnings, and the actual figures are not consistently high, varying from .17 for wool textiles to .85 for motors. They are at least all positive, which is some cause to continue to think that the link between the two is of some importance; on the other hand, since these are correlations for the aggregate of the industry, a positive relation is not a particularly surprising or significant result.

One attempt was made to see whether it was any better to predict what would happen inside each firm over time, rather than to distinguish between firms in each industry: in other words, to do time series analysis rather than cross section analysis. The only difference in doing this would be that the market might not be able to forecast correctly one firm relative to the others, since it might have some irrational feeling about it which affected the price, but it would still be able to predict what would happen to the firm over a period of time. The analysis was attempted for one industry, and was for the short and medium period. (Any longer period was impossible due to lack of observations.) The results were again the same as for the cross section work, since for earnings prediction, the correct sign was obtained only in 50 per cent of the cases, and for dividend prediction the proportion increased to about 60 per cent. Both time periods used had similar effectiveness. Therefore, it seems that the market is just as good or bad at cross section as at time series prediction of growth.

The final conclusion seems to be simply that the market was, in this period, capable of predicting dividend change; but that it was much less efficient at predicting earnings, though even here there were signs of some pattern in the attempts at forecasting. As to the question of the interdependence of these two conclusions, the large dividend cover at the beginning of the period did make it possible for the two series to move somewhat independently, though it is surprising that this appears to happen as much as these results imply. From the point of view of the market, we cannot say that it is actually attempting to predict both of these variables separately. It may be simply forecasting dividends, its small success with earnings being a spurious relationship, caused by the connection between the two variables. In a sense this is a question of no importance, since all we are trying to discover is whether the market is able to predict, not whether it actually is trying to do so. It would be interesting to know whether an investor is concerned with earnings growth, but this interest would only be from a psychological viewpoint; for, when considering the market as an economic organisation, or a place to make money in, the facts that we need to know are those of how the investor behaves, not what he is trying to do.

A question of similar significance, or insignificance, is that of whether the market is in fact predicting the future, or merely reacting to the past. In other words, if market valuation is simply a result of past changes in dividends, and future dividends are related to past dividends, then the successful prediction of the future may really be a result of copying past changes. Again, this is not too vital a question, because even if this were the case, it would imply only that the market uses past dividend or earnings growth as its predicting variable. In the case of earnings, since there seems little or no relation between past changes and future changes, past growth should not result in the yield index predicting future growth due to the link between past and future growth patterns. Since we have just seen that there is only a minimal relation between the valuation of a share and future earnings growth, there is no inconsistancy here. But, in the case of dividends, this relationship may well exist.

Therefore, a second question to be considered is that of how the investor's expectations are formed. Does he use past earnings and dividend growth in order to assess the future of the firm? Can we predict the yield index by using the past financial records of the firms? As before, we have problems of time period. Does the investor consider only the recent past of a company, or is he more interested in what has happened to it over a period of years? This question can be avoided, as in the previous case, by using different periods to find which is the most efficient for prediction.

How important is the question of bias in this second series of regressions? On page 76 we saw that regressing $E(t+1)/E(t)$ on $Y(t)$ would lead to the danger of a positive bias, since we might expect a random increase in $E(t)$ to lead to a decrease in $Y(t)$

due to the effect we are considering in this section; and, therefore, to a positive relation between the variables we are relating to each other. In this section the shortest time period we could use would be to regress $Y(t)$ on $E(t)/E(t-1)$ to see whether the market valuation reacts to the immediate change in the financial situation. A bias could occur here only if there were some relation between $Y(t)$ and $E(t-1)$. This might in fact be the case, since again, a random increase in $E(t-1)$ might lead to a decrease in $Y(t-1)$, and this might effect $Y(t)$ if there is some sticky relationship between these two. However, this would imply either that the investor was considering a longer period, which we can attempt to observe directly, or else was acting in an inconsistent fashion by not revaluing the firm afresh each year. If this latter is the case, then there will be little or no connection between the variables in any case.

The results are presented in Tables 2.3A and 2.3B, using the same definitions of the variables as in the previous case. But, this time, only two periods are used, the short run and the long run. We are attempting to find out the causes of a valuation in a particular year, rather than the average of valuations over some longer period. Therefore, in both periods, the dependent variable is simply $Y(t)$. The independent variable in the short run is $E(t)/E(t-1)$, or $D(t)/D(t-1)$, so that there are ten regressions for each

TABLE 2.3A

Regressions of Yield Index on Growth of Earnings

Sign and significance of Regression Coefficients

		Short run				Long run			
D.F.	Industry	Pos.	Neg.	Sig. Pos.	Sig. Neg.	Pos.	Neg.	Sig. Pos.	Sig. Neg.
35	Miscellaneous ...	2	8	0	1	1	6	0	5
34	Motors ...	4	6	0	0	2	5	0	2
24	Stores ...	4	6	1	2	1	6	0	2
17	Cotton Textiles ...	6	4	0	0	2	5	2	0
26	Elec. Engnrg. ...	5	5	1	0	1	6	0	2
10	Breweries ...	5	5	0	2	2	5	0	0
18	Wool Textiles ...	9	1	2	1	2	5	0	0
25	Building ...	4	6	0	1	3	4	0	0
21	Chemicals and Pharmaceuticals	5	5	0	2	1	6	0	3
19	Paper & Printing	2	8	1	1	1	6	1	2
28	Food	2	8	0	2	0	7	0	5
43	Mech. Eng. (A) ...	3	7	0	1	1	6	0	4
26	Mech. Eng. (B) ...	3	7	0	1	0	7	0	1
	TOTALS ...	54	76	5	14	17	74	3	26

industry from 1952 to 1961. The long period has Y(t) regressed
on E(t–1)/E(t–4), and D(t–1)/D(t–4), with seven regressions for
each industry from 1955 to 1961. As before, the earnings and
dividend figures express the growth of the firm as a proportion of
the average growth of the industry for the same year.

TABLE 2.3B
Regressions of Yield Index on Growth of Dividends
Sign and significance of Regression Coefficients

D.F.	Industry	Short run				Long run			
		Pos.	Neg.	Sig. Pos.	Sig. Neg.	Pos.	Neg.	Sig. Pos.	Sig. Neg.
35	Miscellaneous ...	2	8	1	2	2	5	0	3
34	Motors ...	3	7	1	1	0	7	0	4
24	Stores	5	5	0	2	1	6	0	0
17	Cotton Textiles ...	4	6	3	1	3	4	2	0
26	Elec. Engnrg. ...	3	7	1	1	0	7	0	4
10	Breweries ...	4	6	0	0	3	4	0	2
18	Wool Textiles ...	7	3	2	0	2	5	0	1
25	Building ...	2	8	0	1	3	4	0	1
21	Chemicals and Pharmaceuticals	2	8	0	2	3	4	0	3
19	Paper & Printing	1	9	0	4	0	7	0	2
28	Food	0	10	0	3	1	6	0	4
43	Mech. Eng. (A) ...	2	8	1	1	0	7	0	2
26	Mech. Eng. (B) ...	3	7	0	0	0	7	0	2
	TOTALS ...	38	92	9	18	18	73	2	28

The first impression obtained from the tables is that long run
changes in earnings and dividends are better at explaining the
yield index than short run changes. In fact, in the long run, less
than one-fifth of the coefficients have the wrong sign in both
tables, and about 30 per cent of them are significantly negative.
The results in the two parts of the table are strangely similar
in the long run, perhaps in part due to the fact that in the long
run it is more to be expected that earnings and dividends will
move together, but most likely due to mere chance. In the
short run, the situation is rather different, since dividends are
better at predicting than are earnings, at least in terms of the
signs of the coefficients (with respect to the signs of significant
coefficients the picture is reversed, but this is not such an important
statistic). In both cases the efficiency of prediction is considerably
worse than in the longer run: the proportions of failures being
29 per cent and 41.5 per cent, compared with less than 20 per cent
in the longer period. Again, the pattern of successes between

industries appears to be similar, the best industry and the worst three being identical, and the rest of the pattern not dissimilar.

The main conclusion at this stage must be that it appears that investors take some considerable notice of the past record of a company when deciding what it is worth, and appear to take most notice of the long run movements and somewhat less of the short. However, the comments on bias made on pages [76] and [84–5] should be remembered. These were that there was a real danger of bias affecting the short run results, but not the long. For this reason we cannot say for certain that the short run prediction is in fact any worse than the long.

A second conclusion worth thinking about is that from the results of the long run regressions it would seem possible to predict, with some accuracy at least, the relative yield index one year in advance! This seems to imply that, given the change in dividends over the last four years for the firms in an industry, it is possible to predict the approximate pattern of yield indices in a year's time with an 80 per cent chance of success. Unfortunately, this is not such a profitable discovery as it might seem. In order to use it to predict prices, it is necessary to be able to predict dividends also, since both are required to form the yield index. This cannot be done with 100 per cent certainty. Almost certainly, the losses due to the inaccuracy in predicting dividends, and the fact that we can predict only the very general pattern of the yield index, would nullify the apparent profits to be made.

These results imply that investors do use the figures for the past few years in deciding what the price of a share should be. This fits in with the finding of Mr. Scott who used similar figures (though for one year and all industries), and came up with a negative significant coefficient for the variable of past earnings growth over six years.

The figures for the industry aggregate regressions are shown in Table 2.4.

TABLE 2.4

Inter Industry Regressions of Yield Index on Growth of Earnings and Dividends

		Sign and significance of Regression Coefficients							
		Short run				Long run			
D.F.		Pos.	Neg.	Sig. Pos.	Sig. Neg.	Pos.	Neg.	Sig. Pos.	Sig. Neg.
11 Growth of earnings		3	7	2	2	3	4	3	2
11 Growth of dividends		2	8	1	2	1	6	0	3

The results for the between industry regressions have a similar pattern to those of the within industry regressions, except that the long run earnings figures are markedly bad. This is the same result as that discovered when, earlier, the reverse regressions were shown. It is perhaps worth commenting on this. The fact that it is, or is not, possible to predict within an industry, does not tell us whether it is possible to distinguish between industries. In the former case one is trying to judge the relative ability of the managers of different firms, whereas in the latter case one is mainly trying to predict different movements across the economy. The first is a problem of micro-economics, and the second of macro-economics. Though in each case the attempt at prediction may be based on the same method of projecting past trends into the future, the fact that they seem to work or fail with the same pattern, is not something to be expected for any immediately obvious reason.

Regressing earnings change on the yield index, and the yield index on earnings change, as we have done above, are not to be expected to be completely independent exercises. So it is worth considering the connections between them, in order to see if it is possible to tell whether the similarities and differences are due to economic or statistical causes. Therefore, Table 2.5 shows the number of successful predictions in each of the regressions. In every case the possible total is 17. The industries are numbered in the same order as in Tables 2.1 and 2.3.

TABLE 2.5
Summary of successful predictions in Tables 2.1, 2.2, 2.3, and 2.4
Industries.

	Agg.	1	2	3	4	5	6	7	8	9	10	11	12	13
Regression of earnings growth on yield index	7	13	8	12	6	2	6	10	10	12	13	10	7	5
Regression of dividend growth on yield index	12	11	13	12	11	8	11	16	14	14	15	14	13	11
Regression of yield index on earnings growth... ...	11	14	11	12	9	11	10	6	10	11	14	15	13	14
Regression of yield index on dividend growth ...	14	13	14	11	10	14	10	8	12	12	16	16	15	14

If the industry pattern of success were very similar for the first two lines of the table, as compared with the second two lines, then we would have some reason for doubting the independence of the two types of regression. If they are not independent, then we must worry about the implications of this for the interpretation of what each separately is really showing. One class of regression might be the spurious result of the other. On the other hand, a differing success pattern would lead us to believe that the yield index is decided partly on the basis of past financial results, and then, with the addition of further information, it predicts the future.

It is best to consider the cases of earnings and dividends separately, since there is one big difference between their situations. Thus, in the case of earnings, the prediction of the yield index is markedly better than the prediction of earnings growth (line 3 compared with line 1). Indeed, though it appears that past growth is used as a means of deciding what yield to expect from a share, there is little success in using this yield to predict future growth. This is not surprising in terms of our previous knowledge that there was no connection between past and future earnings growth. But, in an earlier section of this chapter, we discovered a similarity of pattern of success in predicting dividends and earnings. If there is again a similar pattern in using past earnings to predict the yield index, and the yield index to predict future earnings, then this would seem inconsistent with the apparent lack of direct connection between the two. In fact, the simple correlation coefficient between the successes in lines 1 and 3 is only .165, which is so small a figure as to be very probably due to chance factors alone. Therefore, on the earnings side, it seems that the market may depend on past earnings to decide the correct market valuation (especially in the long run as we have seen above), but that it is not good at predicting the future either of the firms or the industries; nor does one's success at predicting market valuation bear any relation to the pattern of success in using market valuation to predict the future growth of earnings.

The problem in the second case, that of dividends, is rather different. Here both regressions are equally good and the question becomes one of whether the yield index tells us anything more than we could learn from directly looking at the past dividend growth. In other words, if past dividends both influence market valuation, and are directly a guide to future dividend growth, then the market valuation, though it does predict future dividend growth quite well, may not tell us anything which is independent of the effects of past dividend growth. One test of this is again the degree of similarity of pattern of successes between different industries. As before, a distinctly dissimilar pattern would suggest that knowledge of the yield index does aid us in foretelling future dividend growth, or to put it differently, that the market must be using other significant information, as well as past results, in predicting the future. In fact, in this case, the simple correlation coefficient between the number of successes in lines 2 and 4 (ignoring the first aggregate column as before) is $-.045$, insignificant and even negative. This latter fact is not surprising, seeing that in industry 7 (namely, wool textiles) the yield index is the most efficient at predicting growth, while past growth is the least efficient at predicting the yield index. Therefore it would seem that the market does use some further information in predicting the future growth of dividends with success, beyond the mere use of past results, though it would be a mistake to suggest that these past results are not important.

It is obvious that many factors do affect market price as well as past and present dividends and earnings, and therefore the above analysis, using only these variables, must be a considerable simplification, so much so that it is perhaps surprising that the results are as significant as they are. However, it seems likely that many of the other variables not included are ones that are of a random variety, and not ones that would improve the efficiency of prediction: indeed, the question is, what further factor could make the prediction of future dividends more efficient than merely using the past results? Perhaps the chairman's statement for year to year changes? Perhaps also, the 'feel' of the market can help to tell what the future of a company will be, or it may use past dividends in a rather more sophisticated way than the mere growth over a fixed past period, measured according to some rigid mathematical convention.

(4) *Conclusions*
The Market and Statistical Problems

As we shall see in Chapter III, attempts to analyse the movements of stock prices have shown little or no success in predicting future prices from present and past prices. The basic finding seems to be that prices follow a random walk model, where the movement of the prices is independent of past movements. However, we seem to have discovered some stronger relation than that, in that future dividend movements are related to the values of the yield index, and also the yield index is related to past dividend and earnings movements. This suggests both that dividend movements through time do follow some sort of non-random path, which is not surprising since dividends are controlled by the board of directors, and also that the yield index follows a non-random path (because the present yield index is related to past dividend change, which is itself related to an earlier yield index).

Does this imply that prices are also connected through time, so that our findings are inconsistent with those of others? The yield index contains two elements that can vary over time: the market price of the share, and the dividend declared by the company. These two variables can be related together in the following three ways: first, they can be completely tied together in that the market immediately adjusts its price to the dividend declared in a rigid proportionate way, in which case only one of these variables could be considered independent, that is, the dividend declared. However, this would imply a constancy of the yield index which, in fact, is not the case. Secondly, they could be completely independent if the market makes no alteration in its valuation of the share as a result of the declared dividend. But, in this case, could we expect to find the results that we have observed? If the price movements follow a random path, and dividends a non-random path, then, to get the observed negative relation between past dividend growth and the yield index, there would have to be a negative relation between past dividend growth and the present dividend level. This seems absurd, because present dividends are expressed as quite arbitrary percentages depending on the nominal value of the share.[1] Therefore, the third possibility, that of the market price adjusting to some extent as a result of dividend changes, must be the case. Here there would be no problem in the dividend changes predicting the yield index, since the mixture of a relationship and a random element in prices would show this result. Moreover, if past changes in dividends are affecting the yield index, then this latter will predict the future changes in dividend, if the dividends are connected over time. But, this third possibility does imply that our results are

---

[1] It may be objected that directors dislike paying high dividend percentages, so that high past dividend growth will result in scrip issues, which in time will cause a low dividend percentage to be paid. This contention is certainly true, but it is not an objection because the analysis in the text works throughout with figures adjusted for such issues.

inconsistent with a strict 'random-walk' movement of prices, for, if there is this relation between the price and dividends even though it is not exact, and if there is also a relation between dividends over time, this implies some relationship in prices over time.

Chapter III will show that there is fairly massive evidence that movements of stock-market prices conform closely with random-walk patterns: but that, nevertheless, there is probably some room for detecting non-random relationships. It should moreover be noted that the price investigations referred to in Chapter III have not been for the U.K. in the 1950s. We may have been dealing with an exceptional period in which the very high initial cover, and high liquidity, permitted dividends to follow an abnormally predictable course, which would have tended to result in price movements being less random than usual.

However, our results, which imply a relation between the yield index and future price growth (since we have found a relation between the yield index and future dividend growth, and since we have found that prices must adjust to dividend growth to be consistent with our results), also apparently contradicts the findings of Mr. Scott[1]. He found no significant relation between the yield index and the change in prices in the following three years.

But even if our results can be accepted only with some reservation, it is still worth considering what they appear to show about the efficiency of the market, and perhaps about ways of using past changes in the financial results of the companies in order to predict prices ahead of the market.

The first question is whether the investor shows any aptitude to foresee what will happen to the firm whose shares he is buying. Here it appears that the yield index does in fact predict at least the direction of relative change in the case of dividends, but the situation is more confused when future earnings are examined. Since it is nonsense to think that the level of dividends can be any indication of their future growth rates, it must follow that there is some adjustment in market price which allows this yield index to predict successfully. Therefore, it seems to be the case that the investor has been able to predict future dividend changes. However, he has not had the same good fortune in foreseeing what earnings will be, although, as discussed at length above, he has

[1] Loc. cit. p. 238.

been relatively more successful in those industries in which he predicted dividends best. This raised the problem of how far it is possible for dividends and earnings to be independent. Obviously in the long run this is impossible. But in the U.K., for the reasons given, the short run was apparently as long as the period investigated.

It is naturally more likely that the investor will be able to guess with some measure of success, when he is trying to decide the future movements of dividends, since he has the directors' forecast for a short period, and they are very likely to follow up their forecast correctly; and, in the longer run, he can assume with some hope of success that they will be bound to consider, with a certain amount of attention, the trend of their dividends continued from the past into the future. On the other hand, the directors do not have much control over their earnings, as shown earlier, and so the investor loses the steadying influence that he could rely on in the case of dividends. It is a little more surprising that he can also predict relative dividend growth for the industries, but cannot do this for earnings. In the case of dividends, again it seems reasonable that on average directors will correctly forecast the future of dividends in their industry, but it seems a little more surprising that the investors are unable to predict correctly that earnings per share in one industry are going to grow more or less on average than in another.

Two of the factors that investors seem to take into account, when deciding what the future of a company will be, are past dividend and earnings growth. These both appear to be of significance for the valuation of shares, because, while moving to some extent independently, they both have some success in predicting the yield index. As for using past results in order to decide profitably what the market price will be, the most hopeful result would appear to be that it is possible, with some degree of success, to use the results over a period of four years to find out the pattern of yield indices for the following year. However, to convert this to price prediction, it is necessary to predict the level of dividends in the following year as well. This should be possible, again using past growth, and the level in the current year: however, by the end of all these calculations, there will very probably be so much inaccuracy that all that will remain is the slight rigidity in the yield index which the market shows. In other words, after all the necessary work, the market will probably have already allowed for the rigidity in dividends that the calculation is based on; so that there will be no chance to make any gain by out-predicting the market.

Economic Conclusions

At the beginning of Chapter I, we said that, from the point of view of society, it is desirable for good managements to be able to borrow on easier terms than bad managements—for this will encourage them to borrow more, and thus manage a larger part of society's new savings.

But we have found that growth performance does not enable one to detect managements which should thus be entrusted with more of society's savings than others. Since the investor has rather little else to judge by, it does not surprise us that we have also found that the investor is not successful in spotting companies whose profitability will increase. Low yielding shares do not on average do better than high yielding shares, so far as earnings growth per share is concerned. While this latter is not a perfect measure of society's benefit, it is probably not a bad one. So we can say that the yield structure established by the market does not appear to perform a beneficial social purpose. It might as well be picked with a pin. But the yield structure is not perverse either. It does not tend to establish high yields for companies which are going to do best, or vice versa. The market is a neutral arbiter. It enables individuals to express their preferences between companies, without apparent harm or benefit to the economy.

It is sometimes argued that it is socially desirable that companies should distribute most or all of their profits. Company directors should not be allowed to direct shareholders' savings to themselves without calling on the market's judgment. This view is weakened, but not necessarily destroyed, by our results. At least the market is not perverse, while it is possible that companies which plough back a high proportion of their profits invest the money at a lower than average return. In the conclusions to the original article we came to the very tentative conclusion that this might be so, this being based on our failure to find a relation between ploughback and growth. But we set no great store by this, for the analysis (pp. 54–8 above) was far from exhaustive.

CHAPTER III

ON THE RANDOMNESS OF STOCK MARKET PRICES

The previous chapters reported the results of our research into dividends, earnings, and market yields. In this chapter we merely report the results of others' work on market prices, and do not include any of our own. However, this restatement of others' findings is important, both to round off our investigation of firms and the market, and also because these statistical findings are not generally known to the investing public as a whole, and may even be partly unknown to the specialists in the field, at least as regards the later results.

The most important articles in this field can all be found in *The random character of stock market prices*, edited by Paul H. Cootner, and published by the M.I.T. Press in 1964. This chapter merely summarizes the main points made in these articles, and explains or avoids the more technical parts of them. If it is desired to find out more about the work done on this subject, then this book is the easiest way to do it, though some expertise in statistical theory is needed to discover the main points put forward. In fact, the book is aimed mainly at the economic theorist rather than the average investor, though there are some strong implications for the latter which we shall point out during the next few pages.

Before summarizing the research done in this field it is perhaps necessary to make the following point. In Chapter II we worked with dividend yields rather than market prices, on the grounds that an investor who is considering a firm's prospects should be concerned with the former rather than the latter, since the latter ignores the income that the investor will get from the share. However, most research done on stock market changes has been in terms of the actual price, and not the yield. This implies an assumption that the investor really is not concerned with income, and buys shares only for a capital gain. This statement is perhaps an exaggeration of the true intention of the investigators, but if they do admit some income motive we would expect them to try and use some form of yield figures[1].

What is the possibility of there being some pattern over time in one of the price or dividend yield series, but not in the other? These two series are mathematically linked by the series for the dividend rate, and, provided that the latter is not itself following a random pattern, it will be impossible for one series to be random without the other also being the same. However, if the dividend series is random, then it would be possible for the price series to be also random, assuming investors are concerned about income, without the yield series being so. It is unlikely that the dividend series will be purely random, but it is also unlikely to contain no random element, and therefore it can be expected to add to the randomness of the price series. If, on the other hand, one believes that the investor is concerned only with price changes, and not with yield, then the above argument can be reversed to state that the yield series can be expected to be more random than the price series. To sum up, any random element in the dividend makes it less likely that we shall be able to find a non-random pattern in the price data, if we assume that it is the yield data that concern the investor; however, if we do find such a pattern, it implies that we should also find some pattern in the yield figures— unless we assume that the investor is concerned mainly with prices, in which case any randomness in the dividend series would weaken the pattern in the case of yields.

So much for the reservation on the significance of the results that follow. The best introduction to the results themselves appears in a paper by Harry V. Roberts, written in 1959 and published in Cootner's book as the first paper. Here he points out, first that charting levels of market prices over some period of time masks the possibility of a random factor in the determination of prices, because such randomness may enter into the *changes* in prices; and, secondly, that these random changes could produce some systematic-looking patterns in the levels.

Chart 3.1 shows the graph of Friday closing levels for one year of the Dow Jones Industrial Index, and might lead to some optimism about finding trends. However, when week to week changes are

---

[1] On the other hand, some, but not all, of the articles in Cootner's book use price series to which the value of dividends has been 'added back', so that the total benefit to the shareholder is reflected in the series.

plotted, as in Chart 3.2, then it becomes very much more difficult to conceive of finding any important patterns. This illustrates the first point. The second point can be seen by simulating a random series. This is done by choosing some average value for the series (0.5), and also for its dispersion or spread (standard deviation of 5.0), so as to make the approximate dimensions of the simulated series near to that of the actual series, and then to plot the series using a random number table having these attributes. The results can be seen in Chart 3.3 which shows the simulated changes in prices, and in Chart 3.4 which shows the simulated market level of prices, both for 52 weeks. Charts 3.1 and 3.4 look sufficiently similar for us to suspect strongly that the actual figures seen in 3.1 could have arisen from such a random walk process, in which case it can only be a waste of time to analyze past results in order to find future price changes.

Of course, Roberts does not intend his argument to be an attempt to prove the case, merely to demonstrate that it is certainly

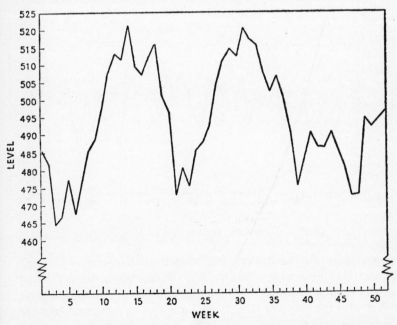

Chart 3.1.   Friday closing levels, December 30, 1955—December 28, 1956. Dow Jones Industrial Index.

H

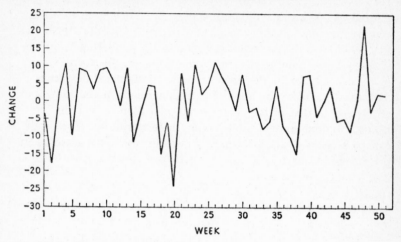

Chart 3.2. Changes from Friday to Friday (closing levels), January 6, 1956—December 28, 1956. Dow Jones Industrial Index.

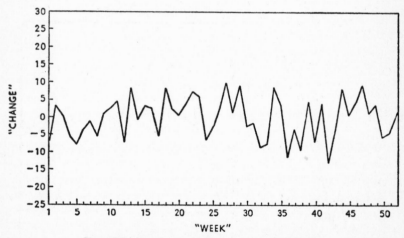

Chart 3.3. Simulated market changes for 52 weeks.

possible at the visual level, and is worth investigating with some care. He also considers two reactions to his results; the first being that, though in the short run chance may be the only significant factor, in the long run other factors must be an important cause of the price changes, such as overall movements in the economy. Roberts admits this possibility, but says that they still need to be

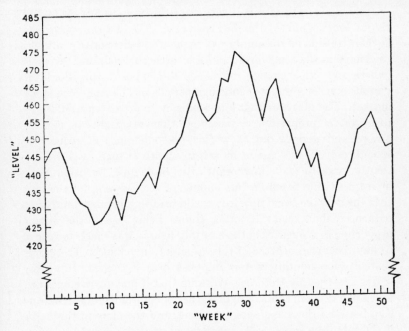

Chart 3.4. Simulated market levels for 52 weeks.

discovered. The second reaction he is more dubious about. This is that we should expect these random results from economic theory, since speculators would notice any non-random pattern there might be, and by acting on this, remove it. But, asks Roberts, why should these speculators remove the patterns? Might not their intervention actually increase any pattern there might be? At any rate it would be desirable to find such behaviour specifically, since it would imply a class of speculator with special knowlege or technique, who would also presumably be very successful. This is a point that we shall return to at the end of this chapter. We might make the further point that the discovery of a pattern *ex post* does not imply that it was predictable.

In any case, what concerns us is whether it is possible to use the price series to find future price changes, without using the special knowledge that these speculators must have. The next stage in the investigation of this comes with the use of relatively simple statistical methods to discover whether price series do deviate from the random walk.

One of the earliest investigations of this was by A. Cowles and H. E. Jones, published in *Econometrica*, 1937. In this paper the authors considered the numbers of sequences (where price continues to change in the same direction for a further period) and reversals (where the price change moves in the opposite direction) for various market groupings and time periods on the American stock market. The idea was that any tendency to a pattern would lead to a greater proportion of sequences than reversals. In fact all groups and periods did show this preponderance of sequences, though only in the case of month to month changes was it sufficiently large to make any profit after brokerage, by using some investment rule based on this finding. Even allowing for the fact that the average trend upwards would lead to a greater number of sequences than reversals, other things being equal, the actual proportion of sequences in the monthly figures was much too great to have occurred because of this, or simply by chance. Therefore, there is some monthly pattern in prices, or so it seemed. However, it was observed by Holbrook Working that if moving averages are taken of a random chain of figures, then there will be some relationship between these averages over time, and therefore in this case, if the monthly figures were averages of daily, or weekly, figures, then the preponderance of sequences could come about even if the underlying series was a random walk. In *Econometrica* 1950 (and Cootner p. 132–8) Cowles revised his original paper in the light of this criticism, and recalculated the sequences and reversals using prices at one date, such as the end day, instead of the averages that he may have used in the earlier paper. Though there is still an excess of sequences, in the case of the monthly figures, the proportion falls very considerably, and with it all hope of anything more than a negligible profit. Indeed, the final excess might be caused merely by the upward trend in prices, as stated earlier. So the first apparent discovery of pattern fades to virtually nothing.

The next important investigation of this problem was done by M. G. Kendall in an article on the analysis of economic time series published in *The Journal of the Royal Statistical Society* (A) in 1953 (Cootner pp. 85–99). The first part of this paper was concerned with commodity markets and need not detain us, but in the second part Kendall analyzed the Actuaries' Index of Industrial Share Prices for the London market for the period 1928–1938.

There are 19 series of weekly figures for various industry and aggregate groupings, changes in which are tested for serial correlation using lags of from one to twenty-nine weeks. In other words, it is tested whether the change in market price this week is related to that of one week earlier, or two weeks earlier, and so on up to twenty-nine weeks earlier. The results are not very encouraging for the investor who would rely on past price data, since most of the series show only an extremely small connection between price changes over time, the only exceptions being certain overall aggregate groups (including the aggregate of all classes), and also stores. Even in the case of these, this positive relation is not very large. Furthermore, Kendall doubted the validity of the results for the aggregate groups, since he pointed out that it was strange that they could show some serial correlation when the individual industries did not. He showed that this could be caused by some spurious relationships over time between the constituent individual industry series; although in fact when he calculated some of these lagged inter-industry correlations, the only ones that came out to have significant size were those with very small or zero lag—i.e., where price changes in industry A this week are similar to those in industry B this week, and mildly connected with the changes in B last week and next week—but for any longer period there is nothing of any size. So it proved impossible to use the price changes of one industry to predict those in another.

Kendall's conclusion is as follows: 'Investors can, perhaps, make money on the Stock Exchange, but not, apparently by watching price-movements and coming in on what looks like a good thing. Such success as investors have seems to be due (a) to chance, (b) to the fact that at certain times all prices move together so that they can't go wrong, (c) to having inside information so that they can anticipate a movement, (d) to their being able to act very quickly, (e) to their being able to operate on such a scale that profits are not expended in brokers' fees and stamp duties.'

Though it is possible to make reservations about Kendall's results in terms of the fact that they do not consider individual firms, and that the period from 1928–1938 was not the most typical from the point of view of observing the market, still these results are powerful evidence of the random walk of stock prices, and make the possibility of the speculator successfully using past price movements for prediction seem very weak.

Arnold B. Moore continued Kendall's work by analyzing the New York market for serial correlation. This was in a doctoral dissertation written in 1960, and published in Cootner pp. 139–161. He initially used the Standard and Poor's 500 Stock Index for weekly figures from 1942 to 1958, and calculated the relation of price changes using a one week lag. (In fact he used the proportional change, whereas Kendall appears to have used absolute changes. Though his method is more acceptable on theoretical grounds, it is not very likely that this would lead to any large difference of results.) As in the case of Kendall's results for aggregates, Moore found some positive relationship, but only a small one. He followed this up by looking at the length of runs of price changes in the same direction, and came to the conclusion that they could well have occurred by chance from a random walk series. So far his results merely confirm those of Kendall and Cowles. But he then proceeded to try something different. He took the weekly prices for a randomly selected sample of thirty stocks on the New York market from 1951–8, and used these to construct his own price index. The main advantage of this over the S. and P. Index is that his was randomly selected whereas the other was not. It is also better for some other more technical reasons. Again he calculated the relation between proportionate price changes lagged by one week, and once more found some weak positive relation. He next investigated the individual firms in the same way, and discovered that the preponderance of these had a *negative* relationship; though this was small, it was certainly significant. This left the apparently strange situation where the index showed an opposite relationship from its component parts. This, however, is not so unusual a phenomenon as might be thought, since the aggregate index reflects overall movements of the economy, and so the positive relation may be caused by the business cycle, whereas the movements in individual prices are presumably also related to the market's appreciation of the firms relative to the rest of the economy. Even so, we need to ask what reason can be given for this negative relation between price changes for individual stocks. Most people would probably expect it to be positive, if anything. Although it is possible to postulate some conditions in the market that could lead to such an effect, it seems more likely that it is once more some form of spurious result arising from the statistical technique used. For, if the level of prices includes some large random element, then, for instance, a large positive random element in the year (1) will lead to an apparent rise in price from the year (0) to (1), and a fall from (1) to (2)—i.e. a negative relation. This effect will be less important in the aggregate series, since the random elements will tend to cancel each other out.[1] Therefore, though Moore's results do reinforce those of Kendall, his further finding is more dubious, as he himself admits.

Therefore, at the conclusion of the research into price patterns at this simple level, we find that the random walk theory is in the ascendant. True, Kendall and Moore did find some small positive relationship for the aggregates, but this was small, and could be caused by movements in the overall economy. For instance, changes in the rate of interest over the business cycle will tend to make prices move in the opposite direction, so as to adjust yields. The result is that a cycle in interest rates over time can lead to a similar movement of prices, and thus to a positive relation for the aggregate, for lags of small size relative to the cycle. In order to detect whatever non-randomness there may be, more powerful statistical methods have to be used. Though these are of interest to the theorist, they are not so important to the investor, and so we will cover the theoretical aspects only briefly, stating the significance of their results for the readers of this book.

One approach, developed by Sidney S. Alexander, involves the use of a filter. He first introduced the idea in the *Industrial Management Review*, 1961 (Cootner pp. 199–218), and revised it in another article published in Cootner pp. 338–72. After an introductory section in the first article, which supported the idea of the random walk, he then discussed a method of observing whether there is such a thing as a trend. The intention is to filter away short term movements of market prices, but to benefit from longer movements. First, a filter size is selected, say 5 per cent. Then, if the price rises by more than 5 per cent, you buy and hold until there is a fall of more than 5 per cent from the highest value reached. At this stage you sell, and go short until the price again rises by more than 5 per cent from the new lowest point reached, when you buy

---

[1] This possible effect, resulting from a random element in the *level* of prices, is not consistent with a random walk in which the probability of any given change of price is unaffected by the previous level. But it is quite possible that some such effect should be operative even where the movement of the series conforms fairly closely to the random walk.

once more. By using such a filter, you minimize the losses when holding shares, or being in a short position, but will be able to obtain the benefits of any larger swings in prices, though losing the benefit of the first part of these swings, which is spent in overcoming the filter. The smaller the filter, the safer the position, and the larger the profit before commission, but since such a small filter will mean a considerable number of transactions, the cost of commission may outway the gain. A very large filter, on the other hand, runs the risk of having larger losses, and losing larger parts of the gains, but since the number of transactions is small, the cost of the brokers' commission will also be small.

The gains calculated by Alexander in the first paper using American aggregate price indices were very considerable. Before commission, with a 5 per cent filter, average profit per year came to 20.5 per cent for 1897–1914, 15.8 per cent for 1914–1929, and 36.8 per cent for 1929–1959. An 8 per cent filter for the same periods yielded 10.5 per cent, 10.7 per cent, and 24.5 per cent. A 15 per cent filter: 6.6 per cent, 9.9 per cent, and 6.9 per cent. A 30 per cent filter: 3.2 per cent, 8.6 per cent, and 7.0 per cent. This was altogether too good to be true, as we shall shortly see. First, it is worth seeing how these results can be reconciled with the random walk findings confirmed by Alexander. He pointed out that all investigations into the random walk had been concerned with movements over some constant time period, while the use of a filter is concerned with the move itself, irrespective of the period taken. Although over time there is a random walk, nevertheless, in terms of the move itself, a shift of x per cent (where x is the size of the filter) is likely to be followed by a continuation of the move by more than another x per cent. (This is necessary to be able to make a profit using the filter.) In other words, there is a tendency for moves themselves to persist, but not for moves to persist *over time*. His conclusion was, 'The riddle has been resolved. The statisticians' findings of a random walk over the time dimension is quite consistent with non-random trends in the move dimension. Such a trend does exist.'

However, the picture was less rosy than Alexander first thought, as is admitted in his second paper. In this he started by examining the various criticisms that had been made against the earlier paper's use of filters. Most of these were not very serious, and do not cause any weakening of the original results. However, there is one question of bias that is very serious. This results from the fact that he used daily closing prices in the earlier paper when evaluating gains and losses from the use of the filters. In fact, of course, there would have been many occasions when there were daily highs or lows that would have triggered off the filter mechanism, but which had been reversed by the time of the closing price, and so did not in fact trigger the filter. On each of these extra transactions there would have been some loss made, since they were swings which did not prove to be long lasting enough to reach the end of the day. Any real use of a filter mechanism would have to use actual price shifts rather than closing prices, and therefore the profit would be less because of this bias. When Alexander recalculated the profits to allow for this bias, they suffered a considerable decrease. For the same periods as before, and before commission, the 5 per cent filter gave average annual profits of 5.3, –1.3, and 11.3 per cent; the 8 per cent filter gave 1.5, 0.0, and 6.9 per cent; the 15 per cent filter gave 2.4, 6.0, and –1.4 per cent; and the 30 per cent filter gave –4.0, 8.5, and 3.3 per cent. This was altogether a less happy state of affairs, since the average profitability of a 'buy and hold' policy would have been 3.2, 14.1, and 3.0 per cent. Only in the last period does the filter method really beat 'buy and hold' at all convincingly, and then only for some filter sizes. Moreover, if commission is allowed for, even this latter period only shows the filter to be as good as 'buy and hold' for filters of the size of 45 per cent! So, it looks as if the use of filters will not be much help in making money on the market. However, as Alexander says, 'The question still remains whether even these profits could plausibly be the result of a random walk. But I must admit that the fun has gone out of it somehow'. He maintained rightly that commission had no bearing on the question of whether a random walk could have produced the results; and that the comparison with 'buy and hold' was misleading, since the comparison with profits due to the trend of prices should be made in some more exact way. When he did compute the filter profits, after removing the element due to the trend in prices, he still found some considerable amount left over (before commission, since this was a theoretical investigation). Therefore, he still concluded that there was some persistence in the movement of the stock price average, but only of a very small amount.

Further points made by Alexander were to note the difference in behaviour of prices before and after 1940, and to compare his concept of a filter with the Dow theory of price movements. This latter, in its most simplified form, is also a filter since it gives buying and selling points by reference to previous peaks and troughs in market prices. The main difference between the two methods is that in the Dow system, the size of the filter varies from cycle to cycle, whereas in Alexander's system it remains fixed. On his computations of the Dow type system's profits, it tended to do better than the similar sized (in terms of numbers of transactions) Alexander filters. Lastly, he evaluated other types of persistence filters, i.e. the number of days that a movement continues, and once more found them more profitable than could be expected from a random walk. His final conclusion was that, although there is too small a consistency for it to be possible to make worthwhile profits after commission, when compared with 'buy and hold', nevertheless there is too much consistency for there to be a random walk in market prices. All these results are for averages of market prices, not for individual shares.

The next two authors in this field can be dealt with more briefly than Alexander, since their work is of less immediate concern to the investor, and of a more technically complex nature. The first to be considered is M. F. M. Osborne who has written two articles on Brownian Motion in the Stock Market. (*Operations Research* 1959 and 1962. Cootner pp. 100–28 and pp. 262–296.) In these papers he compared the movement of stock market prices with the so-called 'Brownian Motion': that is, the movement of molecules. (This movement is simply another form of the random walk, since the movement of molecules depends on chance contacts with the very large number of other molecules in the same area.) In his earlier paper, Osborne examined the price movements in the American market, and saw that the distribution of price changes for various periods was very close to what one would expect if these prices moved according to such random forces. However, he pointed out that it was the logarithm of the price change, rather than the arithmetic value, which followed this rule. This has the rather interesting following conclusion. It implies that there is an equal chance of the same *logarithmic* change in price. Thus it is as likely for a £1 share to move to twice, or half, its present value: i.e., to £2 or 10s. However, investors measure their gains in arithmetic units, and so the gain of £1 is greater than the loss of 10s. Since each of these has the same probability, this implies that a random walk of this type will lead to a secular increase in the arithmetic average of prices. Osborne offered this as an explanation of the long run rise in stock prices, a paradoxical explanation which is independent of the growth in capital assets, or of inflation.

Osborne's second paper, although agreeing with the overall conclusion of the earlier one, was in fact concerned with finding departures from the completely random model. Alexander did this by using the transaction, rather than time, as the base for observing price movements. Osborne also avoided looking at price movements on a time basis, but instead considered the across-the-market dispersion of price changes. In other words, he examined the change in prices for his sample of firms, not in terms of the size of the average price change, but instead as a distribution of price changes. In the first paper, he found that this distribution turned out to be similar to what would be expected from a random process. In the second, he discovered (a) that the higher priced shares, though they have a smaller dispersion than lower priced shares as expected, have in fact a higher dispersion than the theory would predict; and (b) that there is a relationship between the size of this dispersion and the volume of shares traded, again as the random theory predicts, but that this *volume* of shares traded does not follow a random pattern over time, and therefore, presumably, the dispersion of price changes also does not follow a random pattern over time. (Which is not the same as saying that the average value of the price change does not follow a random pattern.) He found a periodicity in the following: (i) the hourly volume of trade; the last half hour was the highest, with a fall through the day from the second highest volume in the opening hour, to a low point just before the final surge in transactions: (ii) the daily volume; for odd lots, a marked increase in volume on Mondays was followed by a decrease on Tuesdays; for the total volume of transactions there was a high point on Tuesdays and Wednesdays: (iii) the monthly volume; this tended to be rising in the autumn, and falling in the winter.

Though these results of Osborne's are of interest in showing that there is at least some pattern in market behaviour, it still does not show a pattern over time in price movements of averages, or of individual shares, and thus it does not show the investor any way to make a profit from the analysis of prices.

One paper, 'Spectral Analysis of Stock Market Prices' by Clive W. J. Granger and Oskar Morgenstern (*Kyklos* 1963, and Cootner, pp. 162–88), does appear to show some pattern in price movements over time. Spectral Analysis is a technique used to examine time series for periodicity by looking at the percentage of the variation over the whole period that can be accounted for by cycles of differing lengths. If the time series follows a random walk path, it is easy to calculate how large a contribution to the total variance each particular cycle should make, and therefore it is possible to see which, if any, contributes significantly more or less than the predicted amount. Thus, if the cycle based on a period of one year contributes more than expected to the overall variance, this means that, over the period, there is some significant annual pattern in prices. This method is an improvement over simple serial correlation techniques in that it shows the whole spectrum of cycles of various periods, and their contribution to the total variation of price; and therefore it is possible to separate out the significant cycles from amongst all the ones of differing length that add up to the observed time series.

Granger and Morgenstern use this technique for various groupings and periods for the New York stock exchange, and obtain the following results. In all cases the overall pattern does follow closely the random walk pattern; but there are certain cycles which show some significantly larger than expected contribution to the overall variance. Before mentioning these, the overall similarity to the random walk must be again stressed. These results do not show a strong cyclical pattern of price movements, but, rather, a barely noticeable pattern as follows:

(i) Weekly data, 1939–61, for industry groupings. These almost all have a prominent monthly cycle, and most also have an eight-month cycle, which the authors considered to be an indication of the U.S. forty-month business cycle (since eight months is a harmonic of this). . There was also a sign of an annual cycle in some groupings, but this was not so clear. Further, there was an indication of cycles of longer than one year, but the data did not cover a long enough period for this to be clearly seen. The general overall pattern of the various cycles followed here, as always, the random walk model.

(ii) Monthly data, 1875–1956, for aggregate groups. Although there was a slight indication of the forty-month cycle, this was not conclusive. There also appeared to be some cycle of more than five or six years in duration, again too long to be investigated by this method.

(iii) Monthly data, 1946–60, for individual firm prices. Again, all that appeared was the slight tendency towards annual, and eight-monthly, cycles.

The authors also analyzed some volume series but did not find any significant cycles for the over-all weekly sales volume figures. This latter point is in slight disagreement with the findings of Osborne given above, but his strongest results were for periods too short to be shown using the weekly figures of this article.

Spectral Analysis was also used to examine the relation between movements in one price series and another. It was found, for the industry aggregates, and less strongly for the individual firms, that there was some similarity of movements in the series. However, this could not be used profitably by the investor, since there did not appear to be any case where one series led the other, and so it would not be possible to use the movements in the one series to predict similar movements in the other.

The most impressive finding was not these small deviations from the random walk model, which do show some evidence of cycles at work, but rather the way in which, in every case, the actual price series fitted closely the theoretical random walk model. As in the case of Alexander and Osborne, the authors found some deviation from the purely random model, but the deviation was small when compared with the overall closeness of the figures to the random path.

Cootner's own work is of some considerable interest. In an article entitled 'Stock Prices: Random vs. Systematic Changes', (*Industrial Management Review*, 1962, and Cootner pp. 231–52), he developed the idea of price barriers. At its simplest level the theory divides investors into two classes, the majority who have no time to find out the relevant facts about the companies that they are thinking of investing in, and the experts, who have the time and ability to obtain such knowledge. The former would cause a simple random walk in stock prices, except that the latter superimpose some pattern on this randomness. The experts have their own idea of the direction that prices will take, but will act only if the actual price varies considerably from what they consider to be the correct price, since they are concerned to cover the risks involved. From this follows the idea of barriers. Normally the price moves in a random walk fashion (with no serial correlation), but as it reaches the point at which the experts intervene there is a barrier which causes a reversal of the price movement (and therefore a tendency to negative serial correlation). Over the long run the pattern that emerges is the result of the experts' intervention, and not the majority's random transactions. But these experts themselves will cause a long run random walk. Therefore, a random walk will be observed if stock market prices are examined in either the short or long runs. Nevertheless, the experts' superimposed random walk barriers cause a non-random effect in the intermediate run.

This rather complicated theory, which has much common sense to recommend it, even when stated at its simplest level as above, does produce predictions on price behaviour which have been tested to some extent, and confirmed. However, many of these predictions are of a very broad type, which could equally well be produced by other theories. But, since this approach of Cootner's is plausible, and neatly accepts findings of both randomness and non-randomness by other investigators, it has to be taken very seriously. It produces rather similar advice for the investor to that of Alexander, since basically both ignore short-run movements and try to find some longer-run shifts. Alexander did this by using the filter rule to decide whether a particular reversal of price movements was large enough to be considered to be more than a chance fluctuation. One fault of his system was that part of the gain from the movement of prices must needs be lost, since some movement must have taken place for the filter rule to give the buy or sell order. Cootner instead considers some long-run trend as produced by the experts, and when the price moves so far from this as to be unlikely to form part of a random walk of this long-run trend ('unlikely' must be defined beforehand in some probability terms), then it implies that the short-run random walk has moved too far away from what the experts predict, and so they will step in to bring the price back again. Once it has moved back nearer to the trend again, they will stop operating, and allow the market to follow its own short-run devices. Using this method it is possible to predict, and gain from the movements caused by these experts, although both long-run and short-run price movements will still be random. However, there are practical difficulties in actually deciding what the long-run trend is (Cootner suggests using a moving average as an approximation), and in the level of probability to use, and whether to keep it constant. Moreover, his method, since it assumes that the long-run average will follow a random walk pattern does not gain from long run price rises, whereas Alexander's theory does. This, however, merely makes Alexander's theory more applicable to the movement of price indices, whereas Cootner's does much better when applied to the fortunes of individual shares. In order to accept Cootner's theory, it would be desirable to be able, as Roberts says, to identify these experts, who must presumably be very successful.

These then are the writers that have produced the most interesting recent work in the field. There are others doing important technical investigations, but their results do not as yet concern the investor. The final conclusion must be that though the overall picture is one of a random walk in stock prices, there are some reservations on the exact behaviour of this, which can allow some profit to be made, though not as yet of any significant size.

This brings us back to the question of the interpretation of the random walk. It could be a result of either the inexpert, irrational, great mass of investors, according to one hypothesis, or alternatively result from a perfect market where every piece of knowledge concerning the future immediately causes a present price adjustment. In the first case, it would be possible to make money by reacting faster than the market to news of the future; but in neither case would an analysis of past price movements predict future patterns. On the other hand, some mixture of these two extremes would allow the analyst some profit, as seen in the case of Alexander and Cootner. Unfortunately, this can never be large, since, the more the method of analysis is published, the more perfect the market becomes, and the less the chance of profit. Everybody, in attempting to use the same technique, must invalidate the technique itself. So, we are left with the paradox that the only really profitable analysis for the general investor must be one that is not shown to him. In any case, we must suppose that if someone has discovered a really profitable technique of analysis, he would not have been so foolish as to publish it.